For the Love of
Dogs

Chris Walkowicz

Publications International, Ltd.

Chris Walkowicz showed and bred German Shepherds and Bearded Collies with her husband, Ed. She has written nine books and more than 900 articles and columns about dogs and is president emeritus of the Dog Writers Association of America (DWAA). An American Kennel Club judge, she judges more than 50 breeds. Chris has been honored with many awards, including DWAA's Communicator Award and FIDO Woman of the Year.

ISBN-13: 978-1-4127-1278-1

ISBN-10: 1-4127-1278-5

Manufactured in China.

8 7 6 5 4 3 2 1

Library of Congress Control Number: 2005901045

contents

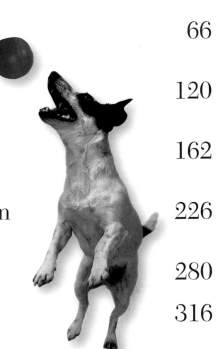

the history & traditions of dogs

"So *they went their way,* and the dog went after them."

—Tobit 11:4, KJV

Creating a Bond

In the beginning, when life consisted only of birthing, eating, doing chores, dying, and few other events, things were pretty dull. Oh, sure, there was the hunt with its danger and excitement, but other than that, the earliest people had little to delight them.

Enter the earliest canid types, hanging around camps to clean up scraps and gnaw on mastodon bones. They eventually went on hunting trips with people, who found that bringing home game was much easier when accompanied by a wolf dog. These early canines circled the game and harassed the animal into position for capture. They even joined the attack, slowing the beast down. And they were happy with the scraps of food people left outside the caves.

These wolf dogs also howled to warn of approaching predators. They were alert to danger and drove other animals away. Cave kids played with the cubs and laughed, and adults found themselves crinkling a smile, too. Those cubs grew to be less shy and could even follow grunted directions. Tribes often found that one or two of the dogs stayed close to a particular family or individual. One fine day, they moved into the caves and slept alongside the people. Ever since, they've warmed our bodies and our hearts.

"Dog: a kind of additional or subsidiary deity designed to catch the overflow and surplus of the world's worship."

—Ambrose Bierce

"His *name is not wild dog* anymore, but the first friend, because *he will be our friend* for always and always and always."

—Rudyard Kipling

"Ever considered what they must think of us? I mean, here we come back from the grocery store with the most amazing haul—chicken, pork, half a cow. We leave at nine and we're back at ten, evidently having caught an entire herd of beasts. They must think we're the greatest hunters on earth!"

—Anne Tyler

"*The truth remains that it was not man who discovered the dog. Rather, it was* the dog who discovered man."

—Stephen Baker

Functions of Dogs

Hunting

Tracking

Chasing

Guarding

Swimming

Herding - - - - - - -

Carrying and towing

Keeping you warm

Companionship - - - - - - - - -

Loving - - - - - -

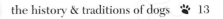

Leap of Faith

Once people realized that dogs were so useful (in addition to being lovable, funny, fascinating creatures), they found if they bred the best herding dog to the next best herding dog, they came up with even better herding dogs! But if they bred the best herding dog to

the best terrier, they wound up with a dog that preferred rounding up rats. Realizing the benefits of getting rid of rats and the possibilities of other canine combinations, people determined to breed type to type. Good thinkers, these cave-dwelling forebears of ours.

Airedale Terrier

Thus came various groups of dogs whose talents combined to make them useful in specific areas. Further refinement came when it was found that even within these groups, some individuals were able to do some things

Bulldog

others couldn't. For instance, an Airedale type could dispatch a larger varmint than a Yorkshire Terrier could (although that Yorkie was determined to try). Over the years, breeds were developed. At least 35 breeds, as diverse as the Bulldog and the Great Dane, came from the mastiff type alone!

Though the Romans recognized six different types of dogs, purebred dogs as we know them did not exist. During Roman times, *dogs were still used primarily as aides in the hunt and in war.* Yet even then, toy dogs existed for the pleasure of their owners. And it is from the Romans that we get a warning that is still seen today: *Cave canem,* or Beware of the Dog.

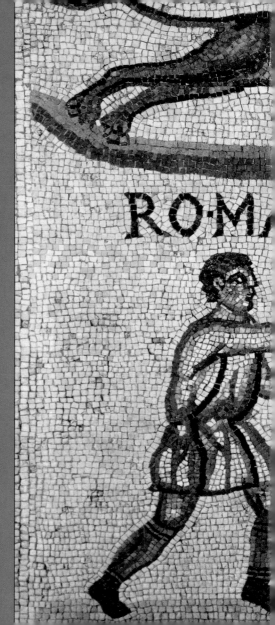

Types of Dogs

Guardians

Herders

Mastiffs

Bird flushers⌐

Hunters

Sighthounds - - - - - - - - - - - - - -

Scenthounds

Terriers

Nordics - - - - - - - - -

Learning Together

The earliest people had various talents. Some were hunters, and others prepared the game for food. Still others made clothing from the pelts. A few experimented with plants and discovered how to cure ailments—or kill an enemy. Some people developed tools to make life easier: a travois, a wheel, a mallet. And there always seemed to be a great chef or two around who knew which herbs and spices would jazz up the wooly mammoth stew.

Wolf dogs also began to display attributes well suited for specific duties. Some were bold and aggressive in protecting the people and area around their fireside. Others used their noses to find game, which meant humans no longer had to endure futile searches for animals that had already moved on to greener pastures. Larger wolf dogs threw their bodies into pulling the travois, loaded with great hunks of meat and skins. They were cheered on by those people who had previously done this burdensome chore themselves.

When keeping more docile animals such as sheep or goats was deemed useful, some wolf dogs were used to gather these animals together and keep them from wandering. Still others protected the flocks and herds from predators. Rodents and reptiles that stole food and generally made life bothersome were driven out and killed by wolf dogs that hung around the cave. These dogs would even dig into the terra firma and drag these creatures out, quickly dispatching of them with their sharp teeth.

The dog-headed god Anubis was worshipped by ancient Egyptians.

"The *greatness of a nation* and its *moral progress* can be judged by the way that its *animals are treated.*"

—Ghandi

Wide, Wonderful World of Dogs

People around the world had different needs for dogs, depending on the climate, the flora, and the fauna. For instance, desert tribes needed sleek, swift dogs that could survive in hot, arid climes—dogs that could dash across the sands to capture an elusive hare. On the other hand, natives of Siberia needed a strong, furry animal able to tote sleds laden with goods.

Siberian Husky

Barge owners wanted dogs that could fit on their vessels to keep them free of vermin and also bark to warn of trespassers. Shepherds demanded dogs that would round up sheep and keep them safe from harm. Herding dogs needed thick coats to protect themselves, not only from inclement weather, but also from the sharp teeth and claws of predatory animals.

Dogs that lived in forests needed different coats than those that lived in plains. Those that dwelled on the plateaus had different needs than those that lived in the mountains.

Soon there were different sizes of dogs with different types of coats in a rainbow of colors. There were different pups for different people. And there still are.

Nordic, or Spitz, breeds such as the *Alaskan Malamute* and the Siberian Husky are similar in appearance to the first domesticated dogs. They developed their thick double coats in the harsh climate of the far North and are conditioned to trot steadily over many miles, having been used to haul possessions of the Alaskan and Siberian tribes who bred them.

African Wild Dog

A throwback to ancient dogs, the African wild dog's camouflage blends perfectly into the brush of Africa. Their comical ears give them a unique, quizzical look. They can run at speeds up to 30 miles per hour for as much as three miles—not quite a marathoner, but more than a sprinter!

For family values, they can't be beat—they're considered to be the most social of all the canines. These wild dogs, which are seriously endangered, live in extended families in which all members care for pups and each pack member is treated equally at mealtime. In their advanced social order, a special greeting ritual marks all comings and goings. Only the dominant male and the dominant female breed. The others are just nursemaids and wannabes.

American Kennel Club Groups

The American Kennel Club recognizes more than 150 breeds, which fit in to seven groups. More than 400 breeds exist throughout the world.

Sporting

Working

Hound

Terrier

Non-Sporting

Toy

Herding

The Rarest AKC Breeds

English Foxhound ----

Otterhound

American Foxhound

Sussex Spaniel

Harrier

Skye Terrier -------------

Finnish Spitz

Dandie Dinmont Terrier

Sealyham Terrier ----

Plott Hound

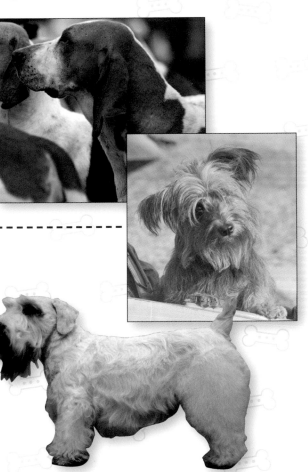

Companionship

In addition to the delight of their company, dogs were found to have other benefits, among them, according to one 15th-century writer, *"to bere awaye the flees."* Little dogs accompanied the elite everywhere to be of comfort, to be caressed, to be displayed, and to rid their owners of those pesky biting bugs.

Royalty adopted *the canine craze,* and dogs were set for eternity. This meant our furry friends not only had to turn spits, keep away rats (and fleas), and supply our supper, *but they became our friends.*

It was only natural, humans being the competitive spirits we are, that one dog was compared to another. Some of the dogs were just, doggone it, cuter or prettier than others—at least in their besotted owners' eyes. Other dogs performed certain tasks or tricks better than their rivals. And so dog shows were born.

Awaiting Carriage
by Salvador Barbudo-Sanchez

The Poop on Shows

Dog shows are popular almost everywhere. Some, such as Crufts, Westminster Kennel Club, and Morris and Essex are known and respected throughout the world. Other smaller shows may serve just their own communities or towns. But regardless of the size or prestige of an event and no matter where in the world it may take place, every dog show has certain basics to cover. Some shows have a different focus than others, but each one comes down to dogs being judged in a number of categories over a variety of criteria. Throughout this chapter, you'll read what you need to know about dog shows.

In the Middle Ages, only the wealthy were permitted to keep hunting dogs. Poor people who owned such dogs were either taxed heavily on ownership or were required to lame the dogs so they couldn't be used to poach game on noble estates. It wasn't until the Industrial Revolution brought about increased employment and income that middle- and lower-income families could afford to keep dogs. Not surprisingly, this is when many of today's popular pet breeds were developed. Many of these new breeds had no specific purpose; they served only as companions.

the history & traditions of dogs 🐾 33

"Depending on his breed, *the dog is considered*

loyal, brave, resolute, pugnacious, ever-obedient, dependable, alert,

lovable and fast—to name just a few of his sterling qualities."

—Carrie Shook

No matter how dogs differ in appearance or purpose, their behavior is what bonds them as a species. Although individual dogs have unique personalities, all dogs communicate in similar ways, with wagging tails, doggie grins, barks, and play bows. From the *Great Dane* to the tiny Yorkie, each dog is genetically pro-grammed to relate to other dogs and people in this easy-to-learn body language.

Conformation

Each national breed club has a "Standard" of the ideal dog, from its earset, nose size, and teeth alignment to the set of its wagging tail. Judges determine which dog in each class most closely resembles this ideal from their interpretation of the Standard. Conformation judging is, therefore, subjective. Male and female classes are held separately, and the winner of each class returns to the ring for the "winners" class of each gender. The winner of this contest receives Championship points and goes on to compete with dogs that have already attained the title of Champion. The ultimate winner is named Best of Breed (BOB).

Next, the many BOB winners compete in one of seven various groups. The first-place winner of each group meets the other six group winners and competes for Best in Show. Thus, it is basically a process of elimination in which each dog remains a competitor until it is beaten by another.

Competition is sorted by classes that are separated by gender except for Best of Breed, in which both genders compete together. Dogs do not have to begin in Puppy or Novice—they may be entered in Open at their first show if the owner wishes. The title for which they all compete is Champion (Ch).

CONFORMATION CLASSES

6–9 months	American Bred
9–12 months	Open
12–18 months	Winners
Novice	Best of Breed (sometimes called
Bred-by-Exhibitor	"specials" in dog jargon)

Dogs have held many different places in human society. At first, they were merely hangers-on, taking what they could from the strange two-legged creatures. Then they became partners with people in the quest for survival. As the years passed, dogs grew in value, prized not only for their prowess as hunters but also for their good looks. In the late 18th century, owning a certain type of dog, usually a rare one or one of great beauty, was a sign of wealth or status.

"A *dog teaches* a boy *fidelity,* perseverance, and to turn around three times before lying down."

—Robert Benchley

Agility Trials

Agility dogs (and owners) have great fun competing in a canine obstacle course. The agility obstacle course must be completed within an allotted time and with a minimum number of allowable faults. Challenges include a variety of jumps, tunnels, poles through which the dog must zigzag (called *weave poles*), an A frame that the dog must ascend and descend, an elevated dog walk (not quite a high wire, but a high plank), a teeter-totter, and a pause table at which the dog must either sit or lie down.

AGILITY TITLES

Novice A

Novice B (the dog or handler has previously earned title)

Open

Excellent A

Excellent B (the dog or handler has previously earned title)

Titles are consecutive, beginning with Novice, and are awarded in the classes of Standard or Jumpers with Weaves. Dogs may also attain Championship titles in agility.

The Most Popular AKC Breeds

Golden Retriever

Labrador Retriever

German Shepherd

Yorkshire Terrier

Dachshund

Beagle - - - - - - -

Boxer - - - - - -

Poodle - - - -

Shih Tzu

Chihuahua

Though it can hardly be said that the canine species is one to rest on its laurels,
being a show champion comes easily to some dogs. As they say, when you've got it, you've got it.

The status of dogs changed dramatically with the rise of the middle class. In the past, dogs had belonged to one of two categories: working-class animal or pampered prize of the nobility. England's *Queen Victoria loved dogs,* and it was through her patronage that many breeds gained popularity in the 19th century. Led by the queen's example, families of the newly minted middle class began to keep dogs as pets.

In this painting by George Hayter, the young queen-to-be is standing with her spaniel, Dash.

Obedience

Obedience competition begins with Novice dogs and handlers and continues through advanced titles of Open and Utility. Most Novice exercises are performed with the dog on a leash. Open and Utility exercises are performed off leash and include jumps and retrieval work.

OBEDIENCE TITLES

Novice A (exhibitor owns dog and has not achieved an obedience title previously) (CD)

Novice B (exhibitor does not need to be owner and may have achieved titles) (CD)

Open A (dog has not achieved Open title) (CDX)

Open B (any dog/exhibitor that has a Novice title) (CDX)

Utility A (UD)

Utility B (any dog/exhibitor that has an Open title) (UD)

Advanced titles: (UDX, OTCh— obedience trial champion)

Titles are consecutive, beginning with Novice.

Purebred Dogs

Bred for years (sometimes centuries) to a specified size, color, earset, coat length, head shape, tail length, and many other characteristics, from instincts to temperament, purebreds come in shapes and sizes to suit everyone. Big or small, hairy or hairless, sleek and racy or strong and substantial—all you have to do is narrow down the choices!

When a breed has produced consistently for many years, you can be fairly certain of the type of dog you're buying. You can have some idea of how large a dog will be as an adult. You can also find out whether regular brushing or trimming will be a requirement or not. Pups often mimic the mother, or *dam*, in temperament, so visiting the litter is a good way to tell whether a dog is child-oriented, protective, outgoing, or laid back. You'll be able to learn whether this dog will be happiest playing catch with the kids, running alongside a bike, or snoring with Grandpa.

For people who wish to enjoy competition or to have their dog produce a litter sometime in the future, purebreds are the only way to go. (Most organizations require registration for events.) Buyers are more likely to contact sellers for a purebred pup than a mix, which they can find at the neighbors' or in a shelter.

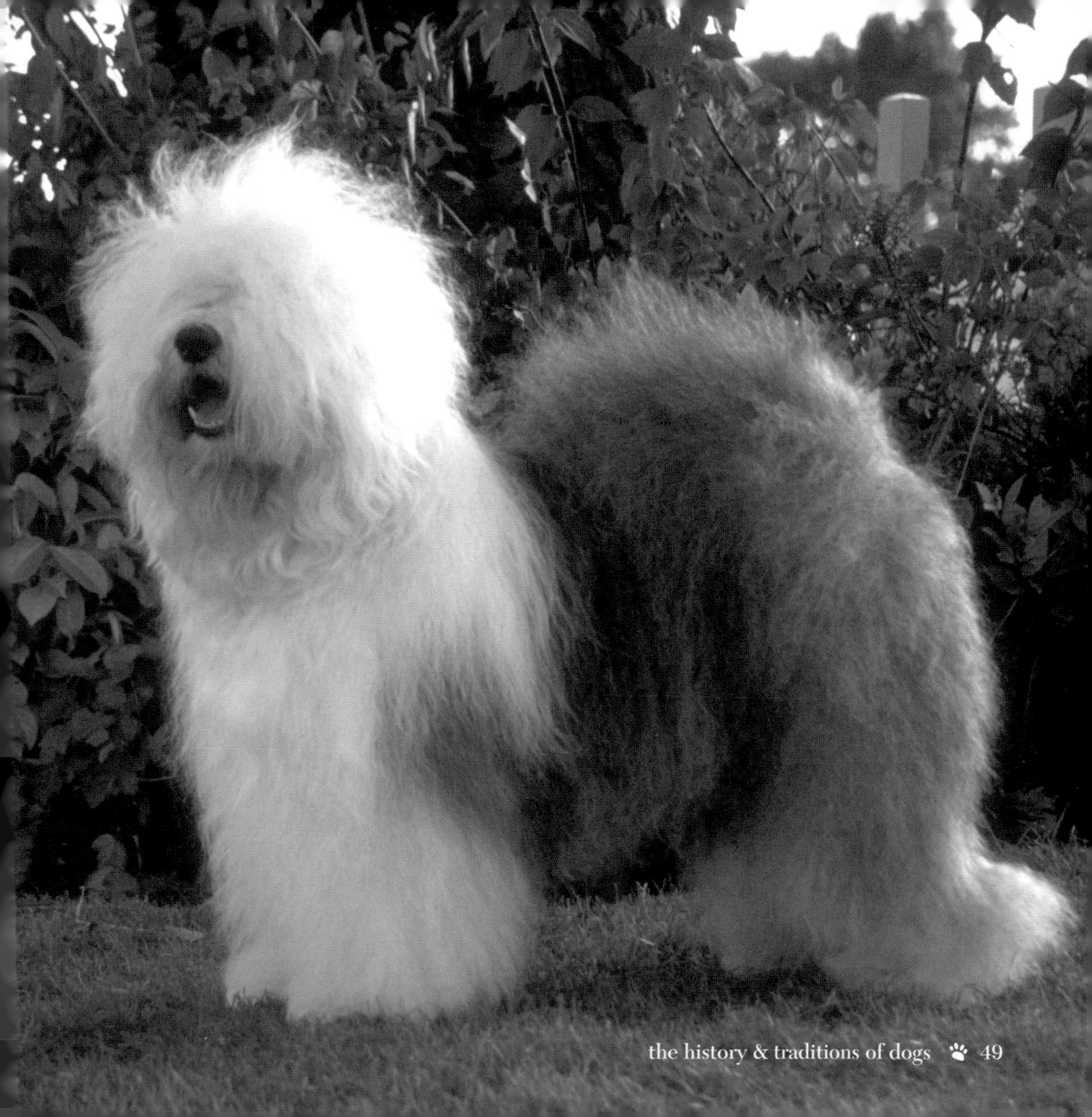

Largest Dogs
(by height)

Irish Wolfhound

Great Dane

Great Pyrenees

Scottish Deerhound

Neapolitan Mastiff

Mastiff

Kuvasz

Black Russian Terrier

Anatolian Shepherd
Dog

Greater Swiss
Mountain Dog

Scottish Deerhound

"A *dog* is the only thing on this earth that *loves you more* than he loves himself."

—Josh Billings

Largest Dogs
(by weight)

Irish Wolfhound

Great Dane

Neapolitan Mastiff

Mastiff

Anatolian

Newfoundland

St. Bernard

Great Pyrenees

Black Russian Terrier

Greater Swiss
    Mountain Dog

St. Bernard

Good grooming is no substitute for good breeding.

Rally

Each exercise course has 10-20 stations with instructions stating the required exercise. The handler and dog walk through the course, performing each exercise as posted, perhaps a three-quarter right turn or left U-turn. The handler must go through the entire course with the dog without waiting for the judge's directions. Rally is less formal than obedience, and the handler is able to talk to and encourage the dog (by clapping hands, patting a leg, or other methods). A command may be given more than once, and precise heeling is not a requirement.

RALLY TITLES

Novice A (RN)	Advanced B (RA)
Novice B (RN)	Excellent A (RE)
Advanced A (RA)	Excellent B (RE)

Titles are consecutive, beginning with Novice.

Smallest Dogs
(by height)

Pomeranian

Chihuahua

Maltese

Pekingese

Japanese Chin

Yorkshire Terrier

Silky Terrier

Papillon

Toy Poodle

Toy Fox Terrier

Chihuahua

Mixed Breeds

Purebred dogs do not always mate with other purebred dogs. Most dogs are mixed breeds of one form or another. Of indiscriminate type and often unknown origins, these dogs need homes and love, too. Mixes can be delightful pets,

especially for people who are not interested in showing or breeding. Many dog owners and would-be dog owners fondly recall a childhood mixed pet that may have wandered onto their doorstep. In that way, mixes frequently provide an introduction to the wonderful world of dogs. But mixed dogs of the same ilk or even the same parents do not always share the same physical or behavioral characteristics. Many times, we don't pick the mixed breed dog—it picks us!

Mad About Mutts

They go by a dozen different names—and not all those names are complimentary. But whether you call them mutts, curb setters, or crossbreeds, there's one thing you can always count on about a mixed-breed dog: No two look alike! One owner says that's what she likes best about them. "It makes me feel special to know no one else has a dog quite like mine."

Pomeranian

Smallest Dogs
(by weight)

Pomeranian

Chihuahua

Maltese

Yorkshire Terrier

Silky Terrier

Papillon

Toy Poodle

Toy Fox Terrier

Japanese Chin

Affenpinscher

Performance Events

Many function-oriented performance tests, trials, and competitions exist for the working dog and the owner who wants to retain that dog's breed instincts. Some breeds perform particular tasks more effectively and easily than others. Herding dogs, such as Border Collies, German Shepherd Dogs, Old English Sheepdogs, and Welsh Corgis, compete in herding livestock under the guidance of a handler. Sighthounds, such as Greyhounds, Borzois, Irish Wolfhounds, Whippets, and Afghan Hounds, take part in lure coursing events in which they follow a lure around a set course and are judged on agility, endurance, speed, enthusiasm, and following ability. Earthdog events are available for terriers and Dachshunds bred to "go to ground" in the hunt, to seek out quarry such as badgers or rats in their dens and tunnels. The American Kennel Club has recently added coonhound events to its roster. Descended from scenthounds used to track foxes and other game, coonhounds, such as Bluetick Coonhounds, Plotts, and Black and Tan Coonhounds, were bred to track and tree raccoons. Today they can compete in field trials, night hunts, water races, and other contests to show off their abilities.

Blessing of the Animals

St. Francis of Assisi wrote, "All praise to you, Oh Lord, for all these brother and sister creatures."

Many churches now offer a blessing of the animals, often held to celebrate the feast of St. Francis on October 2. At larger churches, the line may look like that of the animals entering Noah's Ark.

The blessing is often the following:

"Blessed are you, Lord God, maker of all living creatures. You called forth fish in the sea, birds in the air, and animals on the land. You inspired St. Francis to call all of them his brothers and sisters. We ask you to bless this pet. By the power of your love, enable it to live according to your plan. May we always praise you for all your beauty in creation. Blessed are you, Lord our God, in all your creatures! Amen."

As part of the ceremony, church leaders will often speak of the unconditional love offered by pets and the reciprocal bond that forms between people and animals.

How to Have Fun with Dogs

Flyball

Flying Disks

Dock retrieval (retrieving off the end of a dock)

Fetch

Canine freestyle (heeling to music or...dancing with dogs)

Jumping -

Mushing

Skijoring/Bikejoring - - - - - - - - - - -
*(with your dog harnessed to
your skis or bike)*

Hide-and-seek - - - - - - - - -

dogs &
their people

"To his dog, *every man is Napoleon;* hence the constant popularity of dogs."

—Aldous Huxley

Lewis, Clark, and Seaman

Captains Meriwether Lewis and William Clark kept journals during their explorations of the Louisiana Purchase territory. Lewis noted the purchase of a "dogg of the Newfoundland breed" for $20. Perhaps due to the breed's aquatic abilities, he named the dog Seaman.

Seaman is mentioned frequently in the journals, which describe him barking loudly at the approach of bears and other intruders, and catching squirrels and deer for the party. Although he received offers to sell his dog, Lewis never considered them.

Seaman had a number of adventures with Lewis and Clark. He was once bitten by a beaver and nearly bled to death, but Lewis stopped the bleeding and saved him. A few days later, while the explorers were sleeping, a buffalo invaded the camp. Seaman came to the rescue and chased the buffalo away. Meriwether Lewis even named a creek after his dog, Seaman's Creek in Montana. Today, however, that creek is known as Monture Creek.

Travels with Charley

At age 58, John Steinbeck decided to chronicle his adventures while crossing the United States, meeting people and seeing life. He had a truck mounted with a camper that he used for work, meals, and sleeping. Steinbeck decided to take his Standard Poodle, Charley (formally known as Charles le Chien), along for company. Steinbeck wasn't the only person who liked a dog for company. A number of drivers like to have a pal in the navigator's seat. Many families include the family dog on day trips and vacations.

Traveling Tips

- Be sure to attach your pet's tags to his collar.
- A permanent ID, such as a microchip or a tattoo (on the groin, not the bicep) is a good idea.
- Check for vaccinations that need to be updated.
- Pack a bag with heartworm preventative, medicine for upset stomach and diarrhea, flea and tick preventative, a favorite toy, towels for cleaning up if necessary, self-rinse shampoo, and clean-up bags.
- Always pick up after your dog.
- Don't let your dog bother other vacationers or campers.
- Always keep your dog on a leash.
- Use bottled water, or bring some water from home, to avoid an upset stomach.
- No fancy food or leftover spaghetti— just the usual menu.

- Accustom your dog to a crate before embarking on the journey. Such an enclosure will ensure the safety of a dog during travel as well as that of the motel staff if you go out and leave the dog behind.
- Never let your dog ride loose in the back of a pickup truck. If he must go in the back, secure him in a tightly anchored crate or with a harness that will not allow him to be thrown out or to jump out.
- Never leave your dog in a car when it's hot outside.
- Heat increases quickly in a car. On an 85-degree day, a car's interior will rise to 102 within 10 minutes—even with windows cracked—and 120 within half an hour. If the day is 90 degrees or hotter, it'll be hot enough in the car to fry an egg, or your dog, by the time you dart into the store and back.

"*Staunch and faithful little lovers* that they are, they give back a hundred fold every sign of love one ever gives them."

—Edith Wharton

One of the *best things about dogs* is that they can *share many of our interests.* Because dogs were bred for so many different purposes, there is a breed that's just right for whatever you want to do—from playing catch on the beach to pulling a sled through snow-covered fields. There are dogs who are best for stretching out beside us on the sofa and watching football, and there are dogs who are best for going outside with us and playing football. Which breed is best for you?

Presidential Pooches

Most presidents have had pets, and many of those pets were dogs. Maybe it's because the presidents needed someone who always looked up to them no matter what. Maybe it's because a dog lover "can't be all bad," an idea that might draw voters. Or maybe it's because they need someone to confide in, someone who will listen and will not judge. Harry Truman once said, "If you want a friend in Washington, get a dog."

President Calvin Coolidge
with his pet dog, Rob Roy

Lifesavers

For some people, the love of dogs goes far beyond their own pets. These dedicated folks spend their time and sometimes their money to save other dogs. Rescuers may work with clubs or shelter groups or may even work on their own. Most national breed clubs have rescue organizations to save and place dogs of their chosen breed in good homes. Some people concentrate on one breed, while others network with various breed clubs. A few branch out to rescue mixes of their own breed. For instance, a group of people interested in Bearded Collies, or Beardies, rescue shaggy dogs they call Neardies.

Ultimate care is taken to find these dogs permanent homes. No one wants a dog to suffer another change or the adoptive family to be disappointed. People who wish to help with rescue can do so in various ways: by adopting a dog that needs a home, by donating funds or participating in fundraising, by fostering a dog or two until a good match comes along, by networking to find good homes, or by transporting dogs to new homes. Several organizations have caravans—one person may drive the dog from New York City to Philadelphia, another from Philly to Louisville, and yet another from Louisville to Little Rock where they meet with the new owner from Dallas.

Rescuers have hearts of gold.

"A dog is one of the few remaining reasons why some people can be persuaded to go for a walk."

—O. A. Battista

Millie

When Tracey got divorced, her ex-husband gained custody of their two Vizslas, and Tracey mourned their loss. While looking for animals to adopt, she saw a Vizsla with a crippled paw. Although others were being interviewed to adopt Millie, when Tracey walked into the room, the dog ran up to her and hugged her as if she knew they should be together.

Millie's leg needed to be amputated, but the dog adapted well. Tracey said, "People say how lucky Millie was to be rescued. My response was always, 'We rescued each other.' Millie made me take my mind off myself, she needed me and I needed her. We both had healing to go through, and the unconditional love between a dog and its human is the best therapy in the world."

One day when Tracey was walking Millie, twin girls approached and asked about the dog. It was a winter day, and the little girls were well bundled with coats and mittens. One of them knelt in the snow and put her hand out to Millie. She said, "Don't worry, you can do anything with one hand. See? I only have one hand, too." She took her coat off to show Millie.

The girls continued to see them now and then and would ask if Millie could swim or play hockey, usually whatever activity the child was considering. Millie couldn't play hockey, but she could help build confidence.

Dogs in the Arts

Dogs are a big part of our lives. Throughout history, they've followed royalty around palaces and been buried with pharaohs. They've appeared in all areas of the arts since the earliest times: carved on cave walls, pictured in paintings, put into movies and television shows. Countless books and songs are written about dogs.

Crufts

The family of young Charles Cruft probably thought he was nuts when he turned up his nose at the family jewelry business and sniffed out another instead. Joining James Spratt in his business, he sold a new product: dog cakes (not a dessert but dog food). Crufts's association with dog breeders on his sales trips awoke a desire to promote dog activities at various exhibitions.

In 1851, he launched his own dog show in Islington, England, which he ran with considerable profit until his death in 1938. His widow continued the tradition for another three years and then asked the Kennel Club (UK) to take over running the show.

In addition to the obedience, flyball, and conformation competitions, vendors are present at the show to tempt you with items you never thought existed, let alone thought you needed. Several demonstrations with dogs, including the amazing and popular Heelwork to Music, are performed. The Discover Dogs event showcases 180 breeds for spectators to become acquainted with specimens of each breed.

After many years in London, the show is now held in Birmingham, England, where it preserves its reputation as "The Greatest Show on Earth."

Basenji

Facts About Crufts

1 **More than 20,000 dogs** from all over the world are entered in Crufts each year.

2 The **show is held** over four days.

3 **More than 130,000 pairs** of aching human feet tread the five halls of Crufts during the show.

4 The **show covers** nearly 20 acres.

5 A member of the British **royal family** often visits Crufts.

6 **Events include:** Discover Dogs, Agility Championships, Obedience Championships, Hero Dog of the Year, Young Kennel Club Competition, Heelwork to Music, Biathlon, Pointer Presentations, Stakes, Show Handling, Flyball, Parade of Vulnerable Native Breeds, Rockwood Display Team, Hearing Dogs for Deaf People, West Midlands Police, Working Trials, Showing and Ringcraft, A Day in the Life of a Dog, Guide Dog Puppy Walking, RAF Dog Display, Senior Handling, Jumping Finals, Paws for Thought Display Team, Duck Herding, Breeder Stakes Competition, Southern Golden Retriever Society Display Team, Gamekeepers Competition, and PAT dog display and conformation.

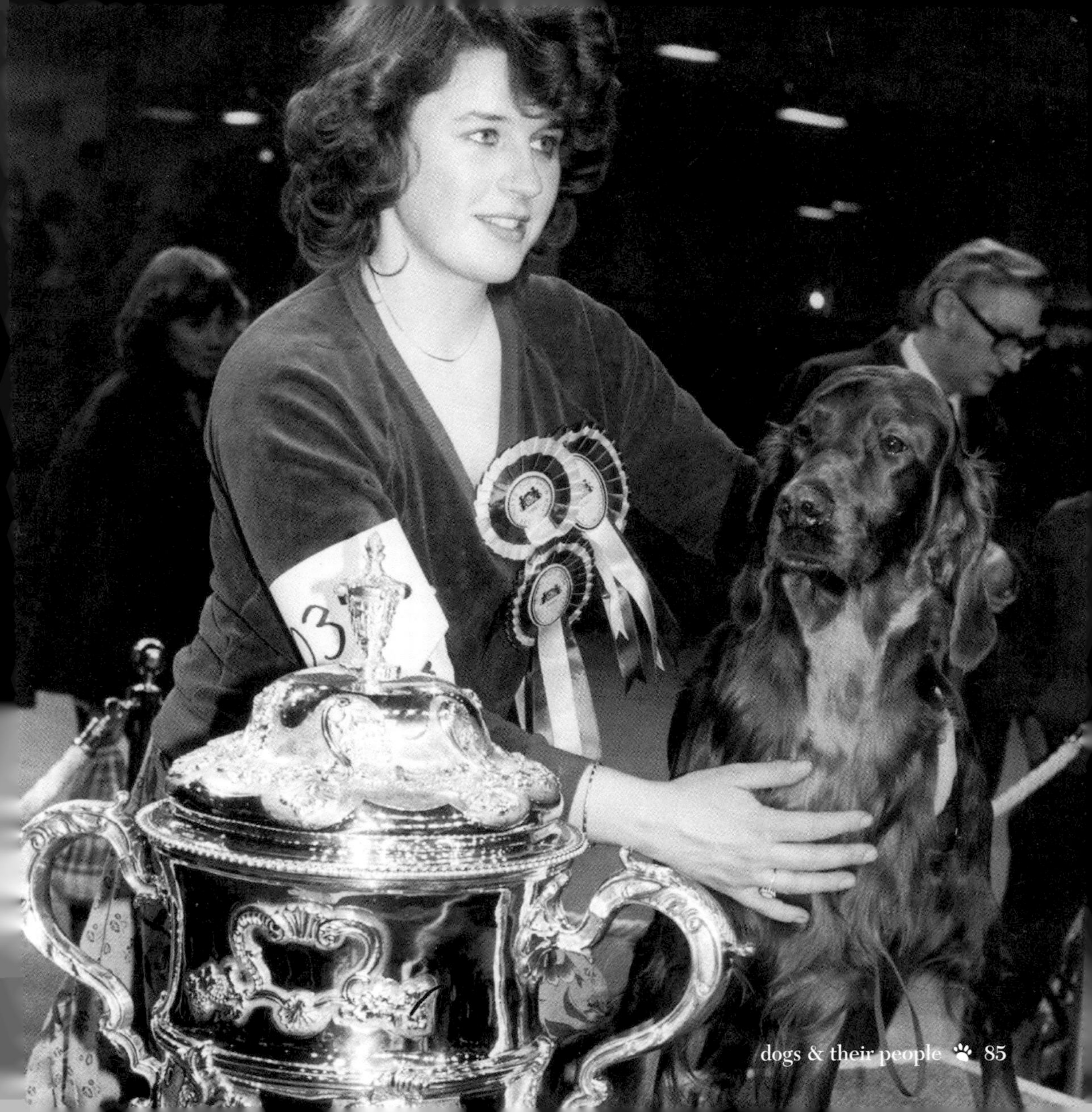

"No one appreciates
the very special genius of
your conversation as the
dog does."

—Christopher Morley

Admiral Wags

Admiral Frederick Sherman's Cocker Spaniel, Admiral Wags, was mascot of the USS *Lexington*. When that ship was hit in World War II's Battle of the Coral Sea, Sherman ordered, "Abandon ship!" He put a life preserver on the dog and

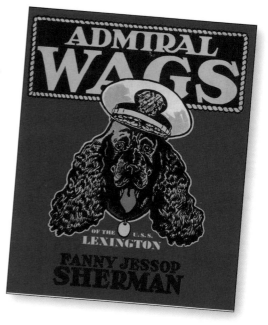

made sure he was taken care of. As commanding officer, he remained onboard until all sailors were off the ship, joining them just before it went under. He and Admiral Wags both survived.

Some First Dogs & Their Presidents

George W. Bush—Barney and Miss Beazley, Scottish Terriers

Bill Clinton—Buddy, a Labrador Retriever

George H. W. Bush—Millie, a Springer Spaniel

Ronald Reagan—Lucky, a Bouvier des Flandres, and Rex, a Cavalier King Charles Spaniel

Richard Nixon—Checkers, a Cocker Spaniel; King Timahoe, an Irish Setter; Vicky, a Poodle; and Pasha, a Yorkshire Terrier

Lyndon Johnson—Him, Her, and Edgar, Beagles; Blanco, a Collie; and Yuki, a mix

John Kennedy—Charlie, a Welsh Terrier; Wolf, an Irish Wolfhound; Clipper, a German Shepherd Dog; Shannon, a Cocker Spaniel; and Pushinka, a mix

Harry S. Truman—
Feller, a Spaniel - - - - - - - - - - - - - -

Franklin Roosevelt—Fala, a Scottie, and Winks, an English Setter

Calvin Coolidge—Rob Roy and Prudence Prim, Collies

Warren Harding—Laddie Boy, an Airedale

Teddy Roosevelt—Pete, a Bull Terrier; Rollo, a St. Bernard; Manchu, a Pekingese; Blackjack, a Manchester Terrier; Sailor Boy, a Chesapeake Bay Retriever; and Tip and Skip, both mixes

Howlin' About Dogs

"Me and You and a Dog Named Boo"

"Where, oh Where, Has
My Little Dog Gone?"

"How Much Is That Doggie in
the Window?"

"Who Let the Dogs Out?"

"Hound Dog"

"B-I-N-G-O"

"Old Blue"

"Old Shep"

"Police Dog Blues"

"Old Dogs, Children and
Watermelon Wine"

Art Show at the Dog Show

The Sunflower Cluster of shows, including the Wichita Kennel Club, Wichita Dog Training Club, Hutchinson Kennel Club, and the Salina Kennel Club, is held annually in Kansas. A juried fine arts competition within the show began in 1986 to celebrate the 50th anniversary of the Wichita Kennel Club. The piece chosen Best of Show is purchased by the sponsors for $1,250 and donated to the American Kennel Club Museum of the Dog in St. Louis, Missouri.

Competitions are held in several categories: oil and acrylic paintings, watercolor paintings, sculpture, jewelry, photography, pastels, drawings, hand-pulled prints, and other media. Several awards are also offered by individuals and clubs, such as best work depicting a terrier or a German Shepherd Dog.

The competition is open to artists 18 years of age or older. All displayed artwork is priced for sale.

Dogs are popular subjects in paintings.

"Man and dog, *an inevitable mix*, is a powerful reason for celebration."

—Roger Caras

"A dog doesn't expect to be treated like a human. *A dog expects a human to act like a dog.*"

—Dr. Bruce Fogle

Few things in life are more restful than relaxing with a good book and a canine friend. *This scene of contentment is commonplace to dog owners,* who enjoy these simple pleasures daily. That is part of the wonder of owning a dog.

Favorite Dog-Eared Books

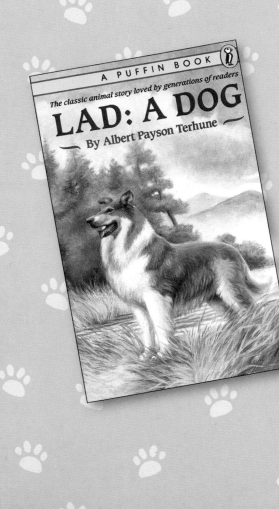

Big Red

Canis

Cujo

The Dog Who Spoke with Gods

Shiloh

Lad: a Dog

The Call of the Wild

Clifford the Big Red Dog

Nop's Trials

A Pedigree to Die For

The Plague Dogs

This Dog for Hire

Pals

Dogs wind themselves around your heart—their love is too great for the little finger. And when you give your heart to a dog, you find all sorts of benefits: You'll have an automatic face washer and plate cleaner; you'll gain the acquaintance of those who stop to admire your pup. Your dog will be a date magnet and will always be happy to do whatever you want and go wherever you want—as long as it includes her.

Your dog won't complain if you wear stripes with plaids. She won't be upset if you flirt with another girl.

Dogs really are your best friends. You can tell them anything, absolutely anything, and they won't think less of you for it. You can confess you like to chew on shoe leather, and they'll just look at you in admiration . . . and maybe even share a shoe with you. Eat an onion-and-garlic sandwich, and they'll think you've got great breath.

You'll never have to go anywhere alone—a gorgeous blonde Lhasa Apso or a tall, dark, and handsome Flat-Coated Retriever will happily join you fishing, dancing, or cloud watching.

Presidential Pooch Pranks

MILLIE'S BOOK

AS DICTATED TO BARBARA BUSH

Lyndon Johnson used to sing with Yuki in the Oval Office.

Kennedy's Charlie and Pushinka had accidental puppies at the White House.

The Bushes' **Millie** had a planned litter (one pup going to their son George W.). Millie authored her own book as well!

Gerald Ford's Liberty and Lyndon Johnson's Him also produced White House puppies.

To end boring meetings or get rid of unwanted guests, Ford trained Liberty to enter a room on a secret signal and begin barking.

Heidi Eisenhower, Grits Carter, and Lucky Reagan were canina non grata after several societal faux paws.

A statue of Franklin Roosevelt's Fala has a permanent post beside the president at his memorial. Winks, FDR's English Setter, once enjoyed a breakfast treat from 19 plates waiting in the kitchen to be served.

Warren Harding's **Laddie Boy** had a birthday party at the White House. Neighbor dogs were invited by the President.

At one time, an official Master of the White House Hounds served on the presidential staff.

Whether walking through flowery fields or along a wooded path, *dogs are constant companions.* They seem to enjoy the sights as much as we do.

A dog is a *great workout companion* for those owners who walk briskly to burn calories, lose weight, and increase muscle tone. Just like their owners, canine fitness walkers must gradually build up strength. Otherwise, it means sore muscles or even an injury, just the same as for humans who begin a fitness program. Once a dog is fit, though, owners will

have a tough time keeping up! When a dog learns to associate the sight of a leash with the prospect of a walk, owners had best prepare themselves for unbridled enthusiasm, including jumps, lunges, and yelps, at the very sight of the leash.

Dogs in Waiting

A Montana shepherd and his Collie, Shep, were inseparable. Unfortunately, the shepherd died and was taken back east by train to be buried. Shep met every train for the next six years, waiting faithfully for his master's return. When he was tragically hit by one of

the trains, railway employees buried him and gave him a marker.

Fifty years later, residents of Fort Benton, Montana, decided this kind of loyalty deserved recognition. They raised $100,000 for a statue of Shep by selling the bricks that support the statue.

In Edinburgh, Scotland, a Skye Terrier named Greyfriars Bobby stood watch at his master's grave for 14 years. When he died, the town erected a memorial to the loyal little dog so that Bobby could continue his eternal vigil.

Art at Sardi's

An American Dog Art competition is held each year at Sardi's restaurant in New York City. It has been hosted by the Dog Fanciers Club since 1988. Categories include sculpture, oils and acrylics, watercolors and gouache, pastels, drawings, prints, and miscellaneous media. In addition, the Dog Fanciers Club holds a luncheon the day after the Westminster show at

which the winning dog is served steak tartar on a silver platter! The judges give a short talk about the dogs in the competition.

Popular author *Dean Koontz* has a treasured Golden Retriever and often includes a dog in his many books. A Golden was a central figure in *The Watchers*.

A Chinese man, Mr. Liu, noticed that his little Pomeranian stood well on his hind legs. First he taught him to balance so that he could more easily blow-dry the dog's tummy after a bath. But one step led to another, and soon the dog, Qiang-Qiang, became known as a dog about town, walking here and there on two legs. He now has little leather booties for his long treks. Qiang-Qiang has walked as far as five miles at a time on his hind legs!

"I came across a
photograph of him not long

ago, his black face with the long snout

sniffing at something in the air, his tail

straight and pointing, his eyes

flashing in some momentary

excitement. Looking at a faded

photograph taken more than forty

years before, even as a grown man,

I would admit I still missed him."

—Willie Morris

The Bush Dogs

Barney was born during President George W. Bush's first term. He's a ball boy, who likes everything from golf balls to soccer balls. He's become quite a video star. He's also infamous for ignoring the President's calls.

Miss Beazley was a birthday gift for Laura Bush from her husband. She was named after one of the favorite childhood books of her librarian mistress. Her preferred treat is a cheeseburger, and she'd rather tantalize Willie the cat than play with big brother Barney. Her goal, according to her official White House biography, is to learn to read by the third grade.

When it comes to sharing their lives with a dog or three, presidents have no advantage over the average American. The latest pet census, conducted by the American Pet Product Manufacturers Association, showed that *74,000,000 dogs enjoy sharing their home with people.*

Up and In—in Beverly Hills

Once upon a time, Drew Barrymore saw a cute mixed breed dog at a flea market, named her Flossie, and gave her a home. But the script doesn't end there.

Flossie repaid Drew's kindness when a fire started in the middle of the night. Barking and banging on the bedroom door, she woke Drew and her husband, Tom Green, in time for them to escape. But that's not the fairy-tale ending either. Cinderella dog Flossie was rewarded with the doghouse of canine dreams when Drew put her mansion in a trust for Flossie.

"You ask of my companions. Hills, sir, and the sundown, and a dog....

They are better than beings, because they know, but do not tell."

—Emily Dickinson

"*My daughter wanted a dog,* and I kept telling her that at my age (87) I did [not] want the responsibility. Then a friend told me about a poor little schnauzer whose owner had passed away and the little dog had been left in the house for weeks with only a daily visit from family to feed and water her. So I said well . . . bring her over, but I really don't think so. In the door came Muffie. She was thin, ungroomed, and looked like a waif. She looked into my eyes, and I knew I had to take this little dog. With her advanced age and mine we immediately understood each other. We took daily walks to the park, had our own special space on the couch, went to bed early, and got up whenever we felt like it. We were two little old neurotic ladies enjoying life together. You never had to worry about her because she liked routine and order. I lost her to cancer and I still miss her till this day, and I will soon celebrate my 92nd birthday. Everyone deserves a Muffie at least once in their life."

—"Muffie's Buddy," from *Wagging Tails Newsletter* Dog Tail of the Month

Forgotten Fido?

Fala captured headlines when it was claimed that President Franklin Roosevelt sent a ship back to pick up the dog after he'd been left behind. The President responded in a speech to the Teamsters Union, "You know, Fala is Scotch, and being a Scottie, as soon as he learned that the Republican fiction writers in Congress and out had concocted a story that I had left him behind on the Aleutian Islands and had sent a destroyer back to find him—at a cost to the taxpayers of two or three, or eight or twenty million dollars—his Scotch soul was furious. He has not been the same dog since. I am accustomed to hearing malicious falsehoods about myself.... But I think I have a right to resent, to object to libelous statements about my dog."

The Franklin Delano Roosevelt Memorial features a statue of Fala.

"*If a dog will not come to you after he has looked you in the face, you ought to go home and examine your conscience.*"

—Woodrow Wilson

Maternal Instinct

A stray dog in Nairobi, Kenya, had a litter of puppies in a shed and had to forage for food to nourish herself while she nursed them. One day, children in the area heard what sounded like a child crying. They found a baby  girl curled next to the mother dog. It seems the dog had found the abandoned baby in a nearby forest and somehow carried her across a busy road and even through some barbed wire to bring her back to the shed. The baby, seven pounds, four ounces, was taken to the hospital and nursed back to health.

Doggone Good Canine Fiction Writers

Robert Armstrong

Carol Lea Benjamin

Laurien Berenson

Melissa Cleary

Susan Conant

Jim Kjelgaard

Virginia Lanier

Donald McCaig

Leslie O'Kane

Albert Payson Terhune

"*Don't walk in front of me,* I may not follow. Don't walk behind me, I may not lead. Walk beside me and be my friend."

—Albert Camus

It's been proven that *petting a dog lowers your blood pressure.*

dogs &
their pals

"*I do love you.* I'm just

not ready to announce it to the world."

"I can't believe we have the same mother."

"We cannot tell the precise moment

when a friendship is formed.

As in filling a vessel drop by drop,

There is at last a drop which makes it run over,

So in a series of kindnesses there is at last

One which makes the heart run over."

—James Boswell

Life in the Pack

Dogs are gregarious, social creatures. They love to be loved! Whether it's fellow dogs, other animals, or humans, they like company. In the nursery, pups wrestle and play with their littermates. If abandoned or stray, dogs will camp on someone's doorstep until they are taken into the fold, or they'll seek out other dogs with which to form a family of sorts.

Canids live in packs with a dominant leader. Right from the start, one pup becomes King of the Hill, while others become either willing followers or rivals for the crown. A regal Beagle or Basset or Basenji often becomes a strong personality when taken out of his litter and placed into a home. The followers usually remain content as long as someone guides them through life.

In our world, a dog's ideal leader is a person and not another dog. With a good leader, a pack lives in harmony. When no one takes charge, life is topsy-turvy and no one has any idea of their role in society. Eventually, whether a true leader or an imposter, someone steps to the forefront.

When two dogs meet, the first order of business is to get to know each other. While the idea may seem uncivilized or even undignified to humans, there are few pleasures more enjoyable to dogs than a good whiff. That's the dog's form of a handshake. Their powerful noses tell them whether the other dog is a male or female and where that dog exists on the tree of life. Is she alpha, a leader? Or is she a follower?

When introducing dogs for the first time, it's best to have both dogs on leash until mutual acceptance is obvious. It's also good to have them meet in a neutral setting rather than on one dog's home turf, where that dog is liable to be more aggressive.

"*One dog barks* at something; the rest bark at him."

—Chinese Proverb

Introductions

Many dogs enjoy having a kindred soul mate. If you're trying to make the transition from being a one-dog family to becoming a two-dog family, be sure initial introductions between the dogs are painless. Although several breeds are so social that gender doesn't make any difference, it's oftentimes easier for an older dog to accept one of the opposite sex. And puppies are less threatening to the resident dog than an adult is.

Try to make the initial introduction in a neutral territory—in a park, at a friend's home, or down the block from the first dog's home turf. If you're buying or adopting a new pup, bring your dog along to begin a friendship before you make a commitment. Be sure both dogs are on leash when they first meet.

Once on home territory, don't leave the dogs loose together when they're alone until you're sure of acceptance by both parties. Confine one to another room, a kennel, or a crate.

Always make sure of the first dog's position in the pack. Most likely, unless she's a comfortable old sweetie who couldn't care less, the

original pet will become the leader. Acknowledge that pecking order by giving the first dog first privileges: the first treat, the first greeting, the first one in or out of the door.

These playmates obviously love their toys. But whether you're talking about people or dogs, who doesn't? *Play is an integral part of the canine personality.* While some dogs are more serious than others, most would give their canine teeth for an afternoon of play. Play begins when pups are barely able to walk and continues into old age. Like children, dogs have favorite toys and will play with them until the toys literally fall apart.

Khaos to the Rescue

Jenette had specifically trained her Border Collie, Khaos, not to chase ducks or to jump in their pond. Khaos became the ducks' self-appointed guardian angel, however, when he saved their lives by disobeying Jenette, not once but twice. The first time the dog flushed out a rat that was stalking baby ducklings. Another time, he began barking furiously at an eel swimming up behind the baby ducklings, dutifully in line behind their mother. Duck pandemonium broke out as the eel approached, but the Collie jumped in to save the ducks. Truly intelligent disobedience!

Khaos the Wonder Dog wasn't just the protector of ducks, however. He and Bailey, a Bullmastiff, were out walking with their owners one morning. It was a windy day, and one of the stick tosses went askew, landing in the river. Bailey fancied herself a retriever and launched herself into the river but was unable to swim back against the current. Struggle as she might, Bailey was fighting a losing battle. Khaos used the current to swim out to Bailey and lead her back to shore.

"I think we are drawn to dogs because *they are the uninhibited creatures* we might be if we weren't certain we knew better."

—George Bird Evans

Dogs invite fun with others in any number of ways, one of which is a play bow: The dog lowers the front half of her body into a "sphinx" position, keeping the rear end raised. The playful dog then stares at her potential playmate and makes small, quick, forward movements as if to say, "Come on! Let's play!" When you see your dog do this, give a play bow back and then start a fun game of fetch or whatever your dog likes to do.

A more subtle invitation to play is a smile. Has your dog ever pulled her lips back horizontally, her jaws slightly opened? In the animal kingdom, this expression means no harm is intended. *A dog's smile is heartwarming,* and very few owners can resist smiling in return.

Dogs also express their desire to play by nudging, pawing, and dancing. A playful dog may sit before her companion, stare, then make downward motions with one front paw. Some dogs are relentless, nudging and pawing an owner until the games begin. For other dogs, the spirit of play is more than they can bear. Don't expect a simple play bow from these dogs! Their entire bodies get in on the action, from the nose to the tip of the tail. They will prance, whirl, twist, and leap to express their desire for fun. It's hard to mistake such exuberance for anything but play.

Talkin' to the Animals

Most dogs are trilingual—they make sounds, mark territory, and speak with their bodies. Vocal communication consists of barking, whimpering, or whining. If owners listen closely, however, they can tell the difference between the "I'm happy you're home" bark, the "I've got to go out *now*" bark, and the "Go away, stranger!" bark.

Dogs (usually males, but sometimes females) mark territory to show they are the boss. The dog who leaves the last or highest mark wins, almost like a canine version of musical chairs.

Body language is easily read by other dogs and by astute humans. A dog that wants to give a warning stands tall, with hackles (hair on the back of the neck) raised. Ears are lifted, and tail and head are held high. This dog is saying, "Don't come any closer." A fearful dog has much of the same body language, but with head lowered and tail tucked.

A confident dog stands her ground with head raised, accepting of touch or approach. The passive dog, on the other hand, stands panting with head lowered, ears held back, and tail wagging. A dog that is submitting to dominance rolls on his back and exposes his stomach. He may have his tongue lolling and tail tucked.

Buddies

Dogs love to play and socialize—whether it be with other dogs, horses, humans, or even cats!

Pups that follow an older dog seem to learn more quickly. The older dog sets the pace and shows the youngster how much fun it is to jump into the pond and retrieve a stick or to roll on his back in the grass. The younger dog can be a fountain of youth for an oldster, quickening his step, cutting naps short, and reminding him of the sheer joy of running.

Scheduled play time is best. Otherwise, the animals are liable to find their own entertainment—and they don't always make the best choices. Scatter the house with toys for two, such as tugs and large balls.

Depending on the breed, supervised play might be advised so that jealousy doesn't cause a fight.

Dr. Doglittle, I Presume?

If you're having trouble understanding your dog, check with KTF Corporation, a Korean company. A translator will communicate with your pet via the phone and will also translate your messages into dogese.

"I always thought that if she had a dog she'd name him Spot— without irony. *If I had a dog, I'd name him Spot,* with irony. But for all practical purposes nobody would know the difference."

—Flannery O'Connor

Talking Dogs

The Taco Bell Dog (Chihuahua)

Lady and Tramp (Cocker and mix)

Fly and Rex (Border Collies in *Babe*)

Lou (Beagle in *Cats and Dogs*)

Hubble (Border Terrier in *Good Boy!*)

Wishbone (Jack Russell Terrier)

Duke (Golden Retriever)

Scooby Doo (Great Dane)

Huckleberry Hound (?)

Goofy (?)

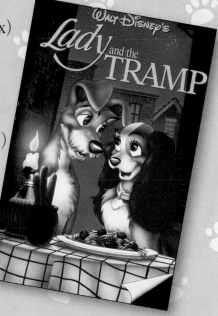

"It's funny how dogs and cats know the inside of folks better than other folks do, isn't it?"

—Eleanor H. Porter

"*The leading distinction between dog and man* is that one can speak and that the other cannot. The absence of the power of speech confines the dog in the development of his intellect."

—Robert Louis Stevenson

For many people, *the love of animals isn't limited to dogs.* Some dog owners are also horse owners, which means that dog and horse often meet. Many horse owners wouldn't think of going for a ride without their canine companion. A horse-rider-dog trio is usually a good mix once the dog learns barn and trail etiquette (don't bark at the horses or get too close to their feet) and the horse learns dog etiquette (don't step on the dog). Trail riding is most fun when a dog tags along.

Dogs and horses have worked together for centuries. Dalmatians are frequently kept in stables because riders know that this breed won't spook their horses. When Australian Cattle Dogs were developed, a dash of Dalmatian was added to their mix in order to achieve that very instinct. The heritage of Jack Russell Terriers is linked to horses as well. Jack Russells were carried on horseback in small sacks and were released during the hunt to unearth quarry from its lair.

"You're cheating again!"

Getting Along

Dogs and cats don't always fight. Some coexist peaceably. Some even become friendly. When introduced at an early age, kittens and puppies are more likely to bond. Of course, certain breeds and individu-

als are more accepting than others. Many dogs have a chase instinct, spurring them to run after things in flight. That flying thing can often be a feline. Early on, kittens and puppies do not have the instinctive fight or flight behavior, and a social family may develop.

"I'll
give
you a
head
start!"

A Kitten's Charm

Dax was a dominant-personality dog who took no guff from her underlings. In a household of dogs and cats, everyone respected her—and avoided her. Thus she had no playmates. One day, her owner rescued a small kitten dodging cars in a parking lot.

Dax took one look at Xena, the kitten, and decided to claim her. The dog protected the kitten from the other animals and washed Xena like a mother. The two even began playing, dashing here and there, with Xena hiding behind the furniture and then pouncing on Dax as she walked past. When they were tired, they curled up together, curmudgeon

and homeless-no-more. Finally, Dax had a friend.

Today Dax's face is showing some gray. But the two are still the best of friends and can usually be found within sight of each other.

"*The dog* was created especially for children. He *is the god of frolic.*"

—Henry Ward Beecher

What's better than one swimming dog? Two swimming dogs, of course. Some breeds, such as the Golden Retriever, take to the water so easily that you might think they were related to the duck. But Goldens aren't the only ones who love the water—many dogs will readily rush into the surf, especially if there's a stick to be retrieved.

"The invitation said black tie and tails."

Gator Wrestling

Every year in the South, alligators go after dogs like gourmands after crème brûlée. Although Coconut, a Lab mix, lived to lick her wounds, it was a close call when an eight-and-a-half-foot, 400-pound gator grabbed her from a supposedly safe pond in a shopping mall. Owners should always keep their dogs on leash in gator country and never allow their pets to swim without first testing the waters. Throwing a pork chop or chicken leg in the pond first just might save your dog's life.

TV Stars

On television, dogs can do almost anything from week to week, from saving lives to making us laugh. Here are a few of our favorites.

Lassie

Wishbone

Backup (from *Veronica Mars*)

Boomer (from *Here's Boomer*)

Comet (from *Full House*)

Pax (from *Longstreet*)

Murray (from *Mad About You*)

Eddie (from *Frasier*)

Quincy (from *Coach*)

Duke (from *The Beverly Hillbillies*)

Bullet (from *The Roy Rogers Show*)

"I'll show you
who's king of
the hill!"

Dogs can remind you that friends come in many different shapes and sizes.

Dogs Driving Us Nuts!

Our best friends can do a lot of things, but driving isn't one of their talents.

In one instance, a devious plot between a herd of cows and a dog smashed a farmer's truck into a tree. How did that happen? Well, Rancher, a Blue Heeler, accompanied his owner to feed the cattle. When they noticed that one of the cows seemed to be ailing, Lyle Sneary left Rancher in the truck and went to check the cow. He got the heifer up and fed her, but all the activity got the attention of the rest of the herd, which decided they were missing out and came at Sneary full tilt. His shouts alerted Rancher, who tried to help by taking things into his own paws. Hitting the gear shift and bumping it out of park, the dog steered the truck smack into a tree. No details are available about whether that stopped the stampede.

Bear, a Newfoundland, sometimes went along on his owner's trash collection run. In one instance, unfortunately, when the owner was loading trash into the bin, he left Bear alone in the cab, and the dog decided to trash the truck by driving it into the river. Glen Shaw was the lifesaver in this case, diving in to rescue his dog.

A three-year-old Bulldog named Harvey took over the controls of a Maserati when his owner, British TV talk show host Johnny Vaughn, got out of the car and walked around it to take the dog out for a walk. Harvey jumped over the Maserati's gearshift and knocked it into drive. He then fell onto the floor and hit the gas pedal. The car crashed into a parked van, and Harvey's owner was stuck paying for damages to both vehicles since Harvey wasn't listed as an insured driver.

Friends Forever

Shorty, a burro, and Bum, a dog, were great friends. Where one was, the other wasn't far behind. They were town mascots in Fairplay, Colorado. When Shorty died, he was given a burial on the court-

house lawn, but his pal Bum refused to leave the site and soon followed his pal to the hereafter. The town put Bum alongside his buddy and erected a monu-ment to the two great friends.

In Sympathy

Dog training classes were set up on a site that once housed a petting zoo. Along with that acreage came an old mated pair of geese named Ozzie and Harriet. The geese had a nice pond, and when the trainers weren't actively training any dogs, Ozzie and Harriet would roam the grassy yards, grazing and munching on snails.

One day while trying to protect his mate, Ozzie was caught and killed by a coyote. Liz was one of the dog trainers, and she worried about Harriet. The two geese, between 20 and 30 years old, had never been far from one another, and now Harriet was alone. Between classes one day, Liz noticed that a one-year-old Australian Shepherd named Bashir had wandered away. She found him lying off to one side, near the goose pond. As she walked toward him and called his

name, Bashir didn't move. Liz soon saw why. Next to Bashir was Harriet, cuddled up to the dog with her head across his back. Bashir's body language didn't indicate that he was afraid—he just didn't seem to want to disturb Harriet. As Liz walked closer, the goose got up and moved away. Apparently Bashir had been able to provide her with some companionship.

For the next few days, Bashir would wander off, and Liz always found him with Harriet. At one point, Harriet even walked up to the training yard, and Bashir met her half way. Sometimes she grazed while he rested nearby, and sometimes they lay side by side. Liz didn't know what brought them together or whether their connection would remain, but on the day when Harriet was grieving the most, a silly puppy provided comfort.

dogs
at work

"I have to walk her *twice*
a day."

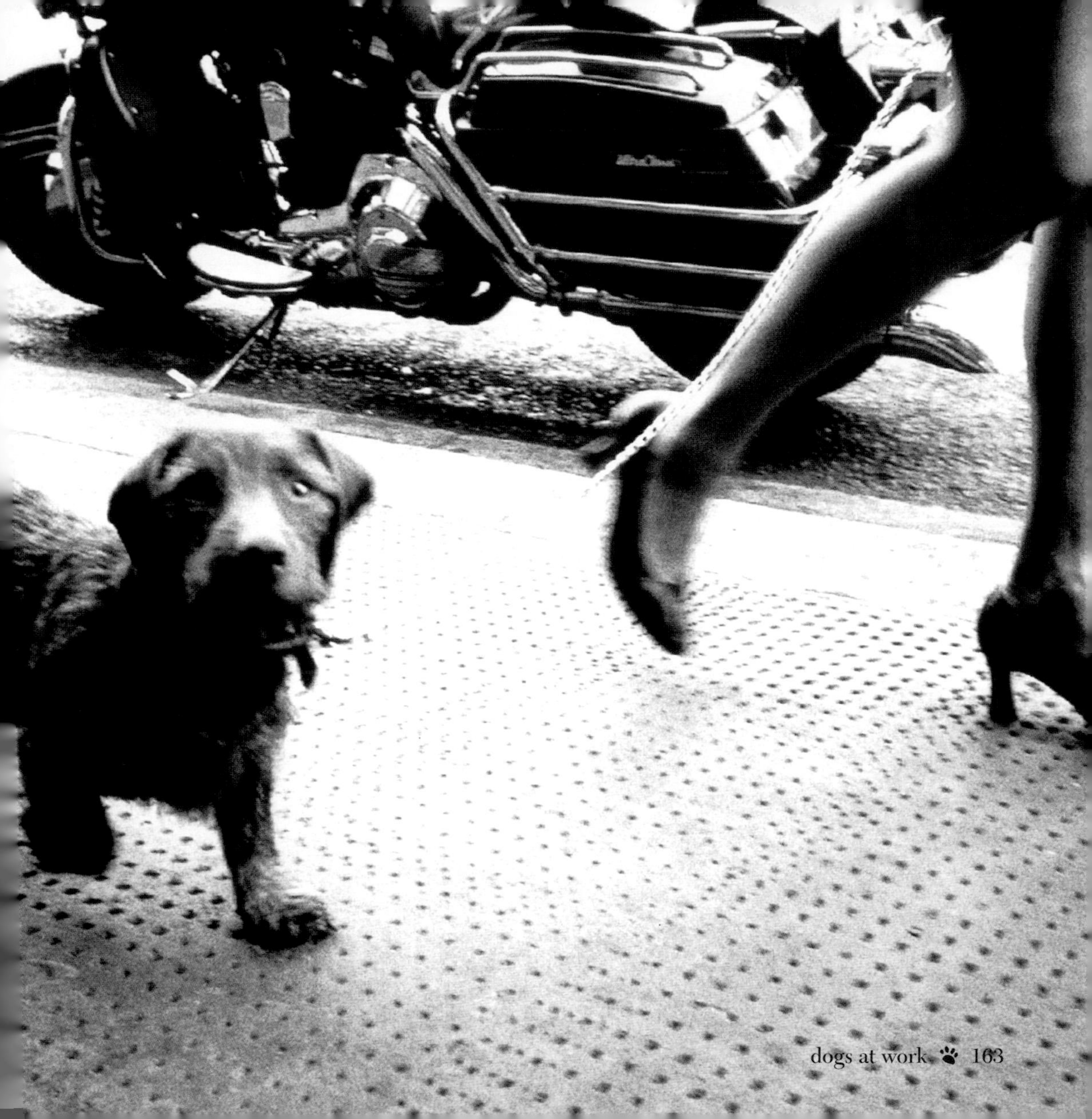

It's a Dog's Life

Although most dogs serve mainly as companions today, they were originally kept for specific reasons—as helpmates to haul supplies, to herd, to guard, to track, to scent game, and to eradicate vermin, for just a few examples. As the years passed, dogs' position in society changed, and they moved into our hearts and homes—and onto our laps and beds. But canines also showed increased working value as they tackled more and more jobs. As the world became more complicated and technical, dogs continued to serve us in various ways, and their eagerness to serve always seemed to lighten our loads. Possessing unique abilities to help those who are challenged, assistance dogs have made lives fuller and more enjoyable.

To a dog, work may just be the following of their instincts: to point birds, to round up livestock, or to retrieve. Their talented sniffers and their desire to please made dogs fit into

many occupations, several of which they continue to maintain today. Although some have reached fame, most are just average workaday Joes and Janes. All of the jobs that dogs perform, they do without a paycheck, strictly as volunteers and for the love of their people. And they don't demand much in return: food, shelter, a bit of play time, and a caress now and then.

Jobs for Dogs

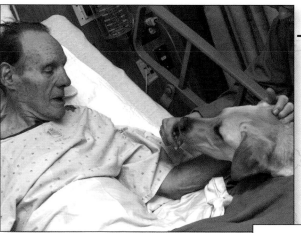

Assistance

Therapy

Herding

Hunting

Drug detection

Border patrol

Police

Military

Sledding

Search and rescue

Police, Military & Government Dogs

These dogs don't wear a uniform, but they serve with the same courage as their uniformed partners. They work in many fields—apprehension, guard work, scent detection, and border patrol. Throughout human history, mastiff-type dogs have been standing guard and terrorizing opposing forces. In recent times, German Shepherd Dogs, Doberman Pinschers, and Belgian Malinois have become favored breeds for guard dogs. It is said that a dog is more likely to intimidate a suspect or a rioting crowd than weapons.

Law enforcement officials use trained dogs for drug detection work or to find accelerants in arson cases. Dogs can also be used to find other contraband, such as plant and meat products brought into the country illegally.

Over the years, military dogs have saved thousands of lives. They're used to detect bombs or land mines, as well as for sentry duty. Military dogs have delivered messages, hauled sleds with injured soldiers, given warning, and perhaps more than anything else, always been dependable companions.

Doberman Pinscher

Surprisingly, this Collie brings only the newspaper—not the paperboy and a few neighborhood friends—to her master. This breed loves to herd…everything. Herding aside, many breeds, including the Border Collie, assist their owners by fetching the daily newspaper. Why do they do it? Some are trained. Others are just helpful!

In the United States and abroad, *sheepdogs assist farmers* in their daily duties, as they have for generations. The farmer and the livestock dog keep a sharp eye out for any members of the flock that might have gone missing. If that ever occurs, dog and farmer search the

countryside, and when the missing sheep is found, a simple command sets the dog in motion to bring in the wanderer. Some sheepdogs live as family dogs, sharing the farmer's hearth. Others live year-round with the sheep, acting as protectors as well as herders.

Sled Dogs

Sled dogs were originally utilized to pull meat and supplies for people who lived in the frozen North. Rather than piling the burden on their own backs, the masters realized that their dogs could not only pull a heavier load and do it faster, but that they seemed to enjoy it. And they'd let their master climb on board, as well! Mostly northern breeds, such as Alaskan Malamutes, Siberian Huskys, and Samoyeds, sled dogs love to run, and they love the snow. But other breeds can participate as well—at least one musher has used Standard Poodles!

A puppy becomes accustomed to a harness early on. Once the puppy is used to the harness, a lightweight item such as a canvas dummy or bumper can be attached, so the dog adjusts to pulling something behind her. Eventually adult dogs learn to pull tires or empty sleds, followed by ones with weights (often their own dog food). Owners can sled with a dog or an entire team for their own enjoyment, or they can enter races. Skiers also enjoy skijoring, in which a harnessed dog pulls them on cross-country skis.

A dog that can pull a sled can pull a sledge or travois on grass. Some dogs also participate in weight pulls, just for the joy of pulling against the harness. They can move amazing weights!

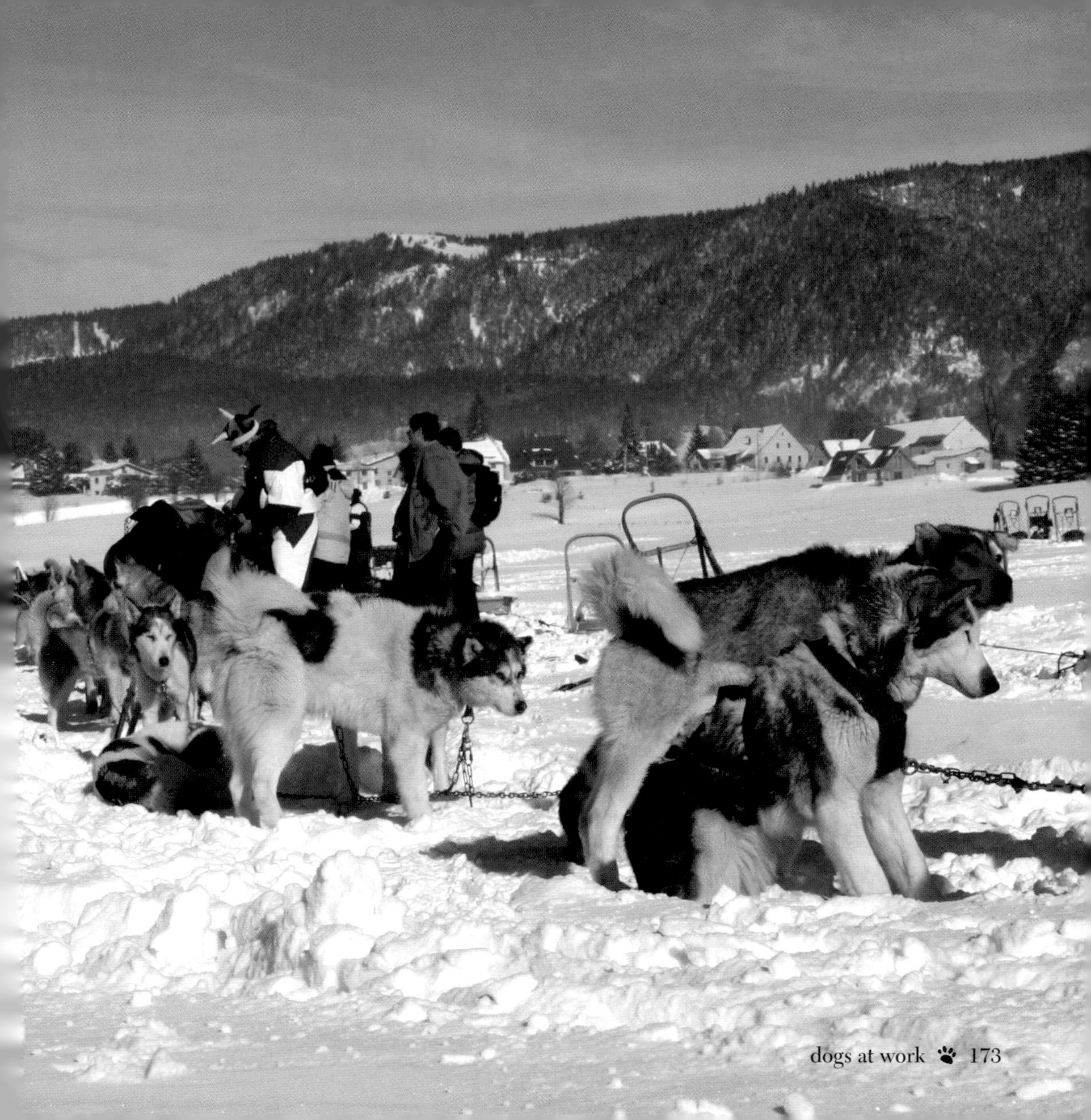

Dogs in War

- Messenger dogs have two masters. The dogs are taught to run between those two masters to deliver messages. They have been used throughout history but are not widely used today.

- Casualty dogs are used to find wounded soldiers.

- Sentry dogs accompany soldiers on their rounds. Due to the canine's keen senses of smell and hearing, these dogs can give warning at anyone's approach. During World War II, 9,300 dogs served as sentries.

- Scout dogs were used extensively in Korea and Vietnam. They walked ahead of the American troops and alerted them to the enemy.

- Tunnel dogs were used mainly in Vietnam to find and explore tunnels built and used by the Viet Cong.

- Mine dogs are trained to detect mines, trip wires, and other explosive devices.

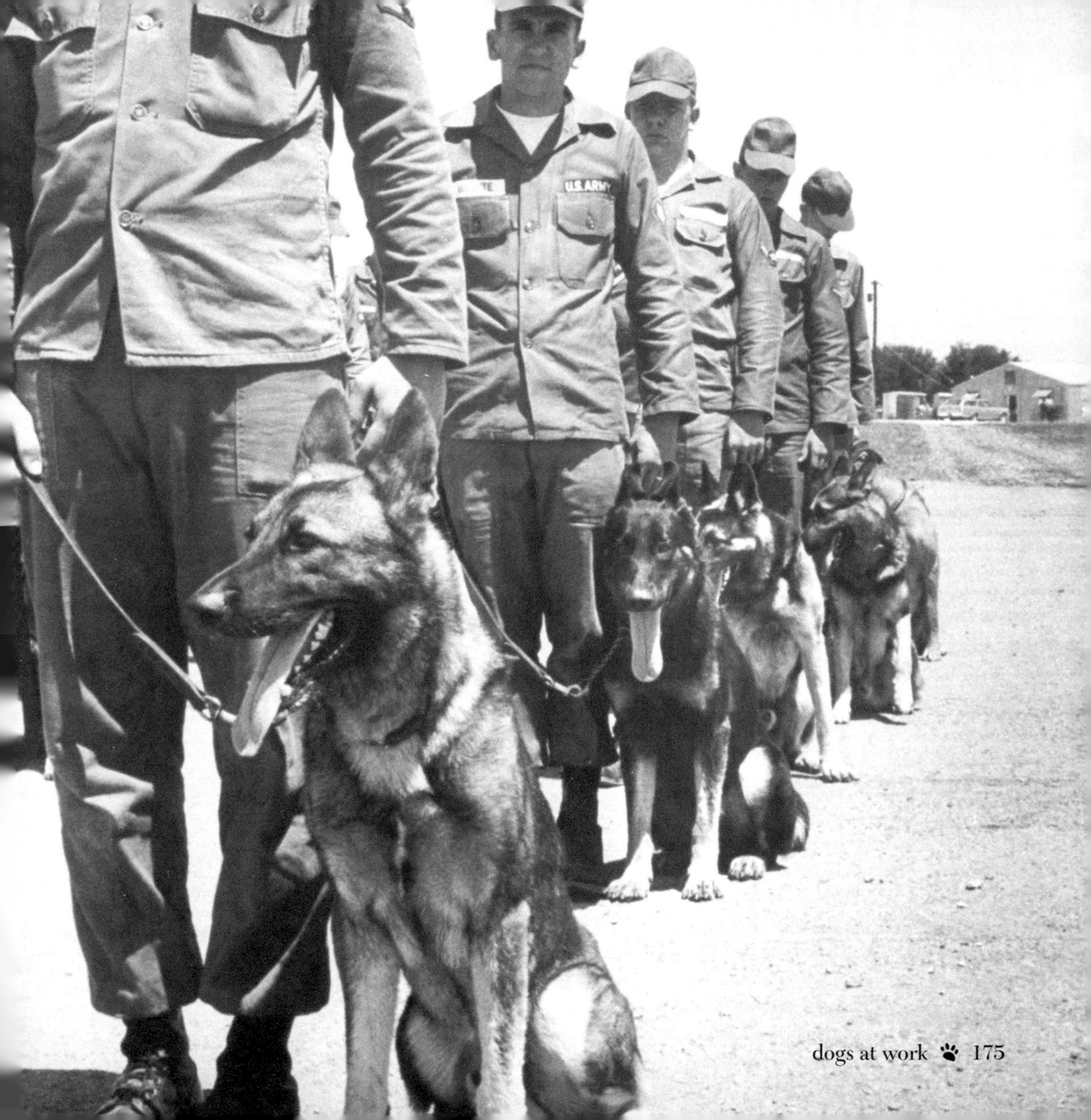
U.S.ARMY

Of all the creatures on Earth, only **the dog has been called "man's best friend."** Many legends tell how that friendship came to pass. In one, it is said that a great earthquake created a wide, deep chasm separating Man and Dog. But when Man called to Dog, the brave animal gathered all his courage and strength and leapt into the chasm, barely making it across and hanging onto the edge for dear life. Man pulled Dog to safety, and ever since, the two have been the best of friends.

In another tale, God commanded the dog to guide humans through perils, ward off their enemies, carry their burdens, and comfort them. So that dogs could accomplish these difficult tasks, God gave them special traits: faithfulness, devotion, understanding, blindness to human faults, and lack of speech to prevent misunderstandings.

Westminster Kennel Club

In 1876, an American tradition was born. Although it was held in Philadelphia its first year, the Westminster show has since resided in New York City and has made its home at Madison Square Garden since 1926.

The show is held over two days, with Working, Terrier, Toy, and Non-Sporting breeds and groups being judged on the first day. Sporting, Hound, and Herding breeds compete the second day, followed by the final Junior Showmanship competition, and the finals of Best in Show. Handlers of the winning dogs appear dressed to shine in these evening competitions, where nerves, pride, anticipation, and excitement wage a battle

The last day of competition at the 127th Westminster Dog Show in 2003.

within each handler and owner.

Long before many homes had televisions sets, Westminster was featured on the small screen in 1948. Now it enjoys top ratings as it's televised live each February. The show has long promoted the sport, as well as purebred dogs and various things dogs and their people can do to help others. After 9/11, search and rescue dogs and their handlers were showcased to the applause and tears of a grateful crowd. Westminster Kennel Club funds a therapy dog program called "Angel on a Leash," which is held in partnership with Morgan Stanley Children's Hospital of NewYork-Presbyterian.

A first-aid kit could save your dog's life if he participates in extreme sports or works for a living. Even if he's a couch spud, this kit could come in handy. A complete first-aid kit for dogs should include a

rectal thermometer, gauze bandages, scissors, bandaging tape, tweezers, antibiotic ointment, a needleless syringe for liquid medication, cotton swabs and cotton balls, hydrogen peroxide or syrup of ipecac to induce vomiting, and activated charcoal tablets to absorb poisons. Other useful items include a blanket and towel, a cold pack or a plastic bag to use as an ice pack, and rubber gloves. It's also a good idea to include your veterinarian's phone number, the phone number of the animal emergency hospital, and a first-aid handbook.

Practicing the piano is so much easier when you've got a sympathetic audience.

The best-known dogsled race—*the Iditarod*—takes place every March in Alaska. Teams race some 1,000 miles through difficult conditions. The annual race commemorates the dogsled relay teams used to rush diptheria serum from Anchorage to Nome to stop an epidemic in 1925.

It could be said that this *Siberian Husky* was born to pull a sled through the snow and ice in subzero weather. Unlike some other breeds that bark more than they howl, Siberian Huskies (like most Nordic breeds) howl more than they bark. Howling is the dog's way of calling the pack—which in many cases is the sled team. In addition to howling for company, dogs—especially hounds—may howl when they have located prey or in response to another dog's howl. Even the sound of an ambulance siren can elicit a howl.

Hunting Dogs

All the dogs in the American Kennel Club's Sporting group—including setters, retrievers, pointing dogs, and spaniels—were bred to help bring home game, mostly birds and small animals. They would find the wounded birds and downed animals the hunter had shot. Almost every country developed its own breed (or several), depending on the prey, weather, terrain, and demand. Some breeds retrieved from water while others found birds in the highlands. Several breeds crashed through brush so the people wouldn't have to, and others performed better in fields.

These hunting breeds continue to follow their instincts today. A number of breeds point the game, some flush it, and several retrieve. A few do it all.

War Dog Memorials

The soldiers who worked with dogs during wartime developed very close bonds with them. They knew they, and many others, owed their lives to the dogs' keen senses and loyalty. Several monuments have been erected to the memory of such dogs, and more are in planning stages.

Guam has a memorial dedicated at the U.S. Marine Corps War Dog Cemetery that portrays a Doberman Pinscher named Kurt who warned of enemy troops and saved the lives of 250 Marines. Names of other dogs who gave their lives for our soldiers also appear on the monument. A replica of the monument can also be seen at the University of Tennessee College of Veterinary Medicine.

The oldest such monument in the United States can be found at the Hartsdale Pet Cemetery in New York City. It is dedicated to the dogs who served in World War I and was built with money donated by the public. The U.S. Air Force Military Working Dog Monument, located at Maxwell Air Force Base in Alabama, contains plaques with dogs' names that were donated by individuals and by several Air Force bases.

Two identical memorials of a soldier with a dog can be seen at March Field Air Museum in Riverside, California, and the National Infantry Museum at Fort Benning in Columbus, Georgia. The engraving on these memorials reads: "They protected us on the field of battle. They watch over our eternal rest. We are grateful."

This monument in New York City commemorates dogs who helped the U.S. Army during World War I.

DEDICATED
TO THE MEMORY OF
THE WAR DOG
ERECTED BY PUBLIC CONTRIBUTION·
BY DOG LOVERS. TO MAN'S MOST
FAITHFUL FRIEND. FOR THE VALIANT
SERVICES RENDERED IN THE
WORLD WAR
1914 — 1918

Westminster

- Westminster is one of the oldest consecutively held sporting events in America, second only to the Kentucky Derby.

- It is one of the few benched shows left in the country, which means spectators can view the breed of their choice any time during the day.

- Entry is limited to 2,500 dogs.

- Champion Warren Remedy, a Smooth Fox Terrier, was awarded Best in Show for three consecutive years, the only dog to achieve that honor.

- Six dogs have won Best in Show twice, the most recent being Champion Chinoe's Adamant James, an English Springer Spaniel, in 1971 and 1972.

- Since 1992, only champions may be entered at Westminster.

- The youngest dog to win Best in Show was a 9-month-old Rough Collie in 1929. The oldest to win was an eight-year-old Papillon in 1999.

- Only two dogs, a Lakeland Terrier and a Kerry Blue Terrier, have won both the legendary Crufts and Westminster shows.

Kirby, a Papillon, shown with owner
John Oulton, wins 1999's Best in Show.

"I brought you the good stuff. I chewed up the junk mail."

"This babysitting is exhausting!"

Popular Male Names

Duke

King

Prince

Max

Sammy

Rocky

Buster

Buddy

Ace

Fido

Although dogs have a wide variety of talents, there are *some jobs* for which they simply *are not suited*.

Chips, War Dog

Chips, a German Shepherd Dog who served during World War II, is probably the best-known poster pup for military dogs. During this time, owners frequently donated their own dogs to fight for the cause, and a man named Edward Wren donated Chips, who was then trained and shipped overseas.

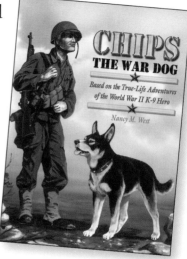

He served gallantly in several different countries and was wounded. He was reported to have attacked an enemy bunker and forced it to surrender. Chips was awarded both the Silver Star and the Purple Heart for his actions. Unfortunately, these awards were later revoked because Chips was a dog.

Dogs in police K-9 units are used for a variety of tasks, including sniffing for bombs. Using their incredible sense of smell, dogs sniff for odors that could signal trouble. Dogs are able to smell things humans cannot. Some dogs may be able to determine in minutes if a bomb is present in a car—it would take a human hours, even days, to perform the same task.

Owney, Maildog

In 1888, a stray dog was found outside a post office in Albany, New York. Postal workers brought him inside, warmed him up, and fed him. He didn't seem to belong to anyone, so they kept him around and called him Owney.

One day, he followed the mail bags to the train and climbed aboard. Evidently, he liked the traveling life, for he spent the next ten years riding from station to station and post office to post office. Moving the mail by train was a recent innovation, and it could be very dangerous. Train wrecks were not unusual, but nothing ever happened to any train Owney was riding. The mail clerks considered him a good luck charm, and Owney became their unofficial mascot.

According to author Lynn Hall, who wrote a book entitled *Owney, the Traveling Dog*, the little dog had a collar that read, "Please return to Albany Post Office." Many of the mail clerks Owney met in railway post offices while on his journeys added medals and tags to his collar. But with all that extra weight from his many destinations, the collar finally became too heavy for Owney, so the Postmaster General of the United States, John Wanamaker, sent him a new jacket to display all of his tags.

When he was seven years old, Owney took a trip around the world by steamship, aided by his postal friends. He traveled across the Pacific Ocean to Asia, and then all throughout Europe—he was met and greeted as a celebrity everywhere he went. When Owney died in 1897, he was stuffed and mounted for display. Today he can be seen at the National Postal Museum of the Smithsonian Institution in Washington, D.C.

Owney is seen here with an unidentified mail carrier in Albany, New York.

One of the first canine occupations, that of gathering flocks and herds, continues today. In addition to being first-rate shepherds, goatherds, and cattle dogs, many breeds compete in trials to retain that instinct—and for fun. If not given the opportunity to round up sheep or other critters, some breeds will find something to herd all by themselves. *Herding dogs* are happiest if given a job to perform.

One of the modern-day uses for herding dogs is that of "goose guard." Beautiful in the air or on ponds, geese can be bothersome pests and even dangerous. Because they don't read signs, geese will trespass onto golf courses and public parks, particularly if there is a pond close by. Goose waste can become a hygienic problem. Even worse, geese have caused accidents by flying into airplane and car windshields. Dogs can be used to patrol the grounds and to scatter the geese to the winds.

Search-and-Rescue dogs are highly trained dogs that lend their paws and noses to disasters of any kind. People use canine talents to track lost children, lead wilderness searches, and seek out survivors and victims of floods, earthquakes, avalanches, and other natural disasters.

It's not only children who get lost, particularly in the wilderness—hunters, hikers, and campers can all become disoriented. Even under normal circumstances, people who become easily confused, such as Alzheimer's patients or the mentally challenged, occasionally wander away from home. Trained Search-and-Rescue (SAR) dogs can also locate cadavers under water or debris. Avalanche dogs have the ability to scent people buried under several feet of snow.

Popular Female Names

Lady

Princess

Duchess

Daisy

Bonnie

Ginger

Molly

Lucy

Maggie

Missy

"All men are
intrinsical rascals,
and I am only sorry
that not being a dog
I can't bite them."
—George Gordon,
Lord Byron

Beagle Brigade

The Animal and Plant Health
Inspection Service (APHIS) has a few
good noses at its beck and call. Beagles,
chosen for their scenting ability as well
as their calm, nonthreatening behavior,
regularly sniff out contraband around
U.S. Customs stations.

Animal products and by-products are not allowed into the country. Also forbidden are certain fruits, vegetables, or plants. Most people simply don't realize these items shouldn't be brought in, or they forget they packed them.

"I'm training for an undercover assignment."

Explosive-Detection Dogs

- These dogs begin training as youngsters, usually between eight months and two years old.

- Reinforcement techniques are used to train the dogs. They are usually given a food reward or allowed to play with a favorite toy when they make a successful find of hidden materials.

- Bombs can contain thousands of ingredients, and the dogs must learn to distinguish between them. Explosive-detection dogs working for the U.S. Marshals Service are trained to recognize as many as 19,000 different kinds of explosives.

- During training, the dogs have about 120 practice sessions per day!

- So that they won't be tainted by outside influences, these dogs spend 24 hours a day with their handlers. Any food they eat comes only from the handlers.

Balto and Togo

In January 1925, children in Nome, Alaska, were dying of diphtheria. Serum was available in Anchorage, but no plane was available to transport it. A train could take it part of the way, but dogsled was the only method of delivering the serum all the way to Nome. Various dogsled teams would relay the serum across the 1,348-mile round-trip.

Musher Leonard Seppala drove a team led by 12-year-old Togo, a 50-pound dog "of muscle and fighting heart." His team raced 169 miles to pick up the serum for the first leg of the relay and then mushed another 91 miles to deliver the precious bundle to the next driver. Sepalla's young assistant, Gunnar Kaasen, picked Balto to lead the last leg of the relay, a total of 106 miles. Although Togo gave his all, injuring his leg, Balto received the accolades for delivering the serum.

Balto was indeed a hero, running through snow, high winds, and dark night while avoiding an icy plunge into water. But Togo, having fought his way over 260 miles of Alaskan winter, was no underdog. He lived to sire many litters, with several dogs today still boasting their lineage back to that dog of heart.

Poor Balto, hero dog, was sold with the rest of the final-leg team to a "dime-a-look" sideshow where they were neglected and possibly mistreated. When the people of Cleveland, Ohio, heard of this, they raised the money to rescue the dogs and bring them to their city, where they lived the rest of their lives at the Brookside Zoo. Balto's body was mounted and is on display at the Cleveland Museum of Natural History. A statue in New York City's Central Park also commemorates the courage of this dog.

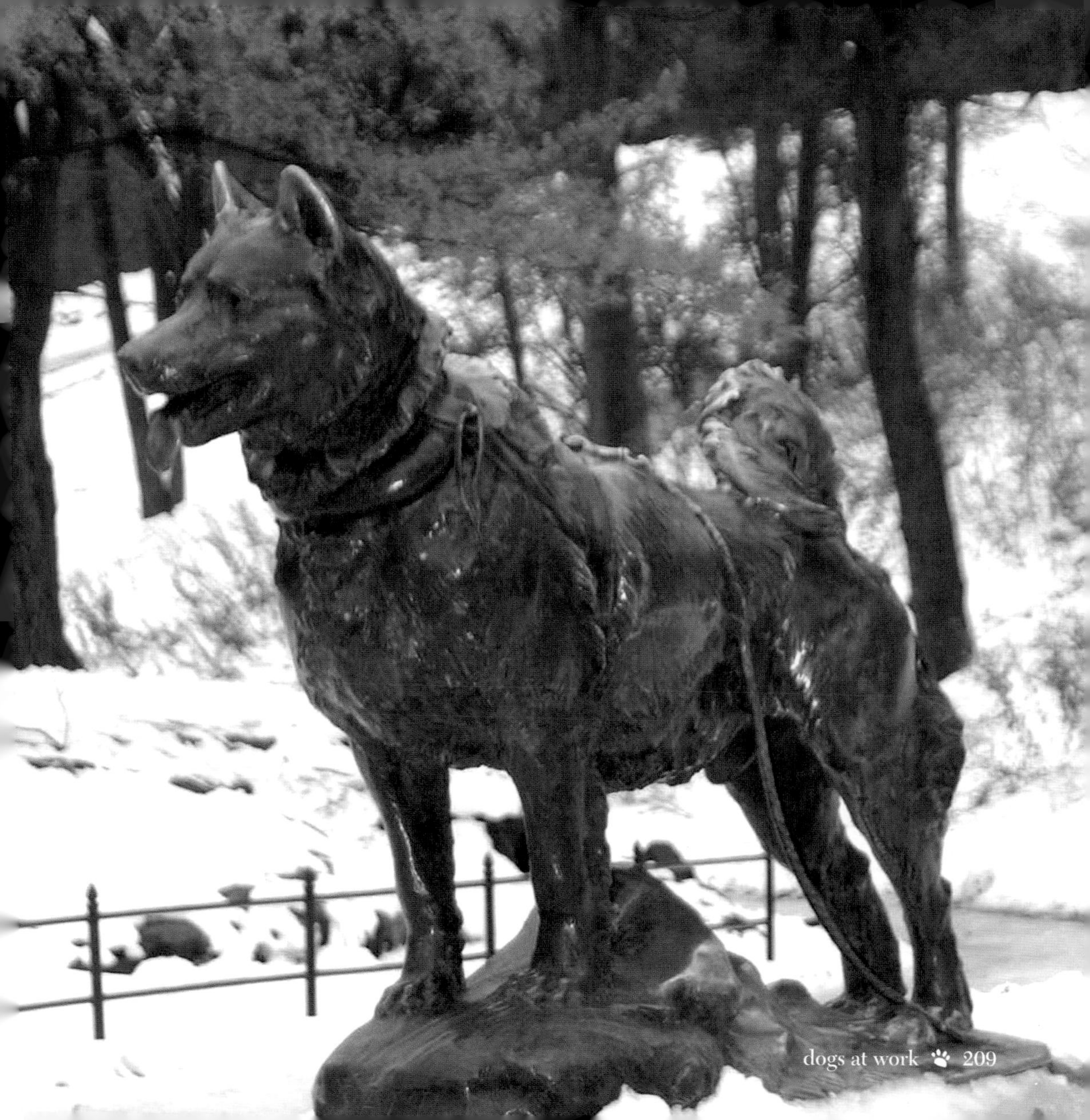

Although its creator, Francis Barraud (1856–1924), lies in obscurity, "His Master's Voice" is one of the best known of all dog pictures, not to mention one of the most frequently reproduced. The painting is said to have been inspired by the artist's pet terrier Nipper, who was terribly puzzled upon hearing the sound of a familiar voice on a phonograph. The Royal Academy rejected "His Master's Voice" when it was submitted for exhibition, but Barraud sold the image to The Gramophone Company after changing the phonograph in the original to the newer-model gramophone that the company produced. American rights to the painting of the famous dog and phonograph were acquired by RCA in 1929.

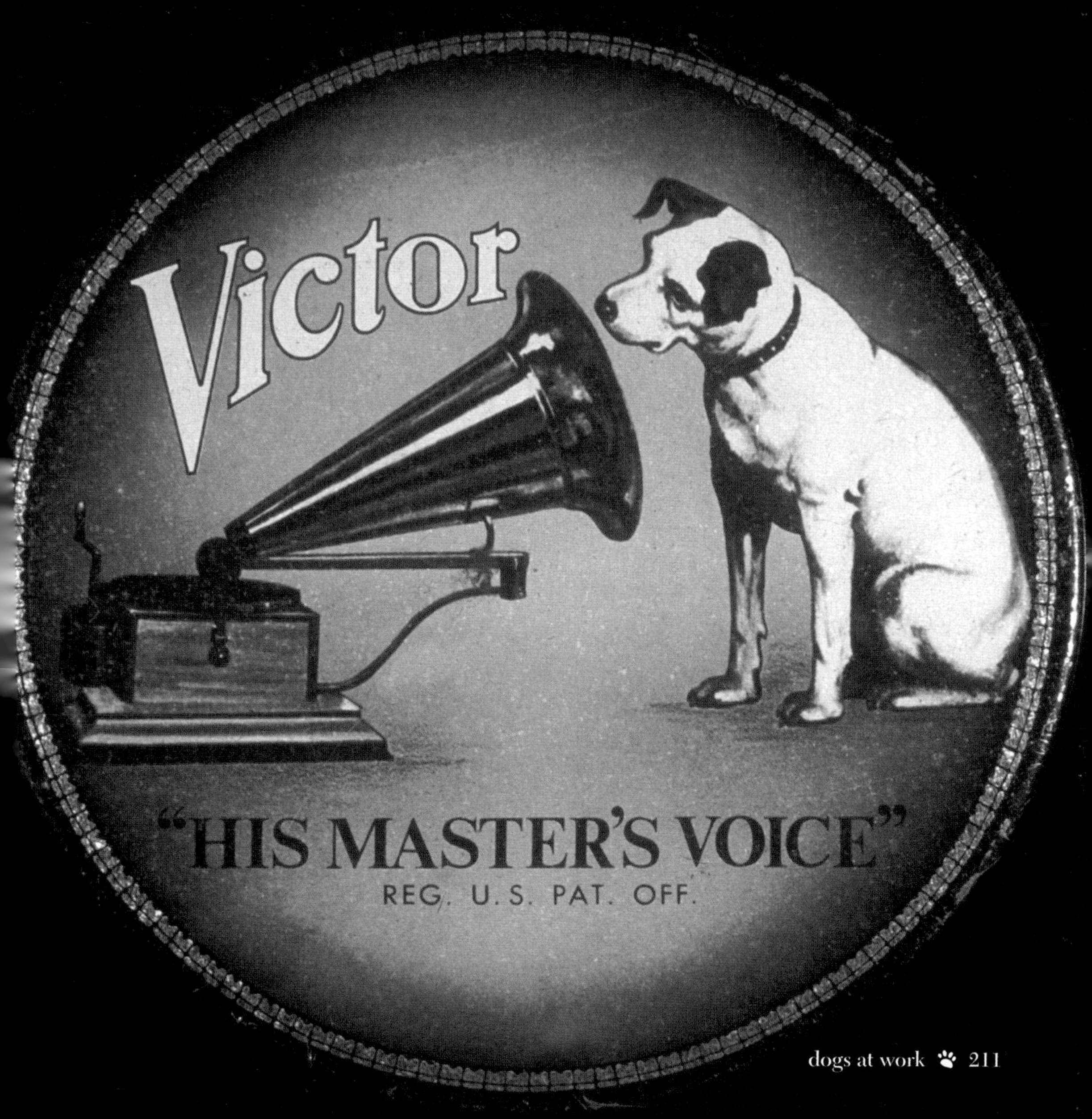
Victor
"HIS MASTER'S VOICE"
REG. U.S. PAT. OFF.

Westminster's Top 12 Most-Winning Breeds

1. *Wirehaired Fox Terrier*

2. Scottish Terrier

3. *English Springer Spaniel*

4. (tie)—
Airedale -
Boxer
Doberman Pinscher
Smooth Fox Terrier
Standard Poodle
Sealyham Terrier
5. (tie)—
Pekingese - - - - - - - - - -
Pointer
Miniature Poodle

The Senses Stats

The dog's sense of smell is its sharpest sense. It is much keener than ours—as much as 100,000 times more powerful! A dog can detect a drop of blood in five quarts of water.

A dog can hear in the range of 67 Hz to 45 kHz. (People are far behind at about 20 Hz to 20 kHz.) That's why they appear at the refrigerator door before we even open it!

Canine vision is not as good as ours, which is why a blind dog can adapt fairly well in a familiar household. Most dogs, however, have better night and peripheral vision than humans do.

Color-blind? Not quite. Being red-green color-blind, dogs view only blue, yellow, and shades of gray, but they probably don't see them as vividly as we do.

This *Chesapeake Bay Retriever* *makes an impressive sight. She seems tensed, ready to pursue game at her hunter's orders. Her form is perfect, her focus intense, and her desire to please overwhelming, which is why this breed is so appreciated. Close kin to the Labrador Retriever, the Chesapeake is also a powerful swimmer and may be happiest when soaking wet. There's no doubt this dog will bring back whatever her master asks her to retrieve.*

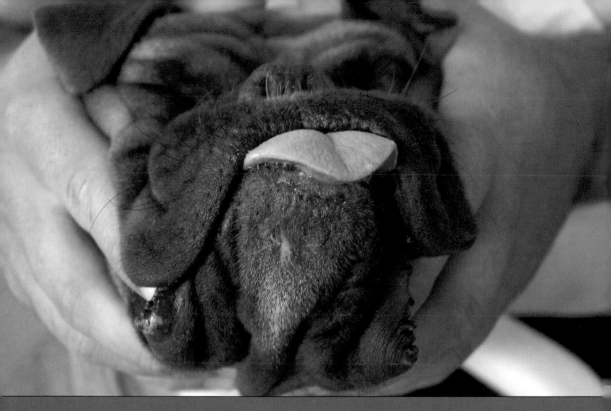

No matter how hard they tried, they couldn't make Buster look like anything but a Bulldog.

"Are you sure Picasso let his dog have a brush?"

"Live to herd" is surely this Border Collie's motto. *Farmers often consider livestock dogs their most important employees—and who wouldn't? These dogs love to work, don't complain, are never late, and never ask for a raise.*

"I'm only waiting tables until I get a callback from Animal Planet, which should be any day now."

Yorkie Doodle Dandy

Smokey, a four-pound Yorkshire Terrier, was found in a foxhole in the jungles of New Guinea. She captured the heart of G.I. William Wynne, who trained her to do a number of tricks. She entertained

the soldiers and accompanied Bill on combat missions—she even used her own parachute. Smokey and Bill continued entertaining people for several years after their return to civilian life. Bill commemorated the mighty canine warrior in a book entitled *Yorkie Doodle Dandy.*

When a canine officer is on the scene, it's not by chance. With exceptional intelligence, a keen nose, and strength beyond compare, a dog is a talented member of a police team. Canine officers can track down, apprehend, and hold a suspect, often more quickly than human officers. These highly trained dogs are intimidating to

even the most hardened criminals—and should be! Off the job, police dogs aren't so fearsome. They often live with their partners as family pets.

"The one absolute, unselfish friend that man can have in this selfish world—the one that never deserts him, the one that never proves ungrateful or treacherous—*is his dog.*

"... A man's dog stands by him in prosperity and in poverty, in health and in sickness. He will sleep on the cold ground, where the wintry winds blow and the snow drives fiercely, if only he can be near his master's side. He will kiss the hand that had no food to offer, he will lick the wounds and sores that come in encounter with the roughness of the world. He guards the sleep of his pauper master as if he were a prince. When all other friends desert, he remains. When riches take wings and reputation falls to pieces he is as constant in his love as the sun in its journey through the heavens. If fortune drives the master forth an outcast in the world, friendless and homeless, the faithful dog asks no higher privilege than that of accompanying him to guard against danger, to fight against his enemies. And when the last scene of all comes, and death takes the master in its embrace, and his body is laid away in the cold ground, no matter if all other friends pursue their way, there by his graveside will the noble dog be found, his head between his paws, his eyes sad but open in alert watchfulness, faithful and true even to death."

—George Graham Vest

dogs just wanna have fun

"My backside smiles

so much, my mouth doesn't have to."

Hiking

From a casual stroll through a neighboring park to a hike through mountains to overnight treks, walking with a dog almost always makes the journey better. But before taking any long walks, the first thing you should do is have your dog examined by a veterinarian and update his vaccinations if necessary.

Start your training with short hikes to build up endurance in both you and your dog. As a hiker, you should always make sure your dog is safe and that other hikers and animals won't be injured or frightened by your dog. Inquire ahead as to whether dogs are allowed on the trails. Dogs should be kept on a six-foot leash when required and have a 100-percent recall rate when off leash in a permissible area. Take water from home for your dog, and don't forget to carry healthy snacks—and meals if you're going on an overnight trek.

Check your dog's feet for cuts or sores, and examine him for ticks when taking a break—or better yet, use a preventative against ticks, and provide booties if the trail is rough. Make sure your dog doesn't chase the wildlife, and be ready to protect him *from* the wildlife, as well.

Many hikers use the dog to carry his own gear: kibble, water, a collapsible bowl, clean-up bags, first aid kit, or a favorite toy. All can be stowed in a doggie backpack. The dog should become accustomed to wearing the backpack and carrying the added weight over a period of time before hitting the Appalachian Trail. (Parts of that trail are indeed open to dogs, but other parts, such as Great Smoky Mountains National Park, are not.)

A Woofin' Good Time!

Competitions

Hunt tests/Field trials

Freestyle

Rally

Agility

Flyball

Road trials

Disk catching

Big air

Lure coursing

Dog shows/obedience
trials

Fetch

Dogs love to pick up things we throw—on dry ground or in the water. Some dogs will actually return the object! Running is great fun and good exercise for them, too. It also expends all that pent-up energy that grows while they wait for you to come home. The best objects for a game of fetch are balls (make sure they're too large to swallow—no golf balls!), sticks, plastic flying disks, and other throw toys.

When Fido ages, he doesn't have to give up his favorite game or spending time with the Best Person in the World. Rolling the ball slowly allows the old fella to toddle after it.

Be sure not to let any dog become overheated or tired when playing—give her something to look forward to. Of course, some dogs, particularly retrievers, will keep going until your arm falls off.

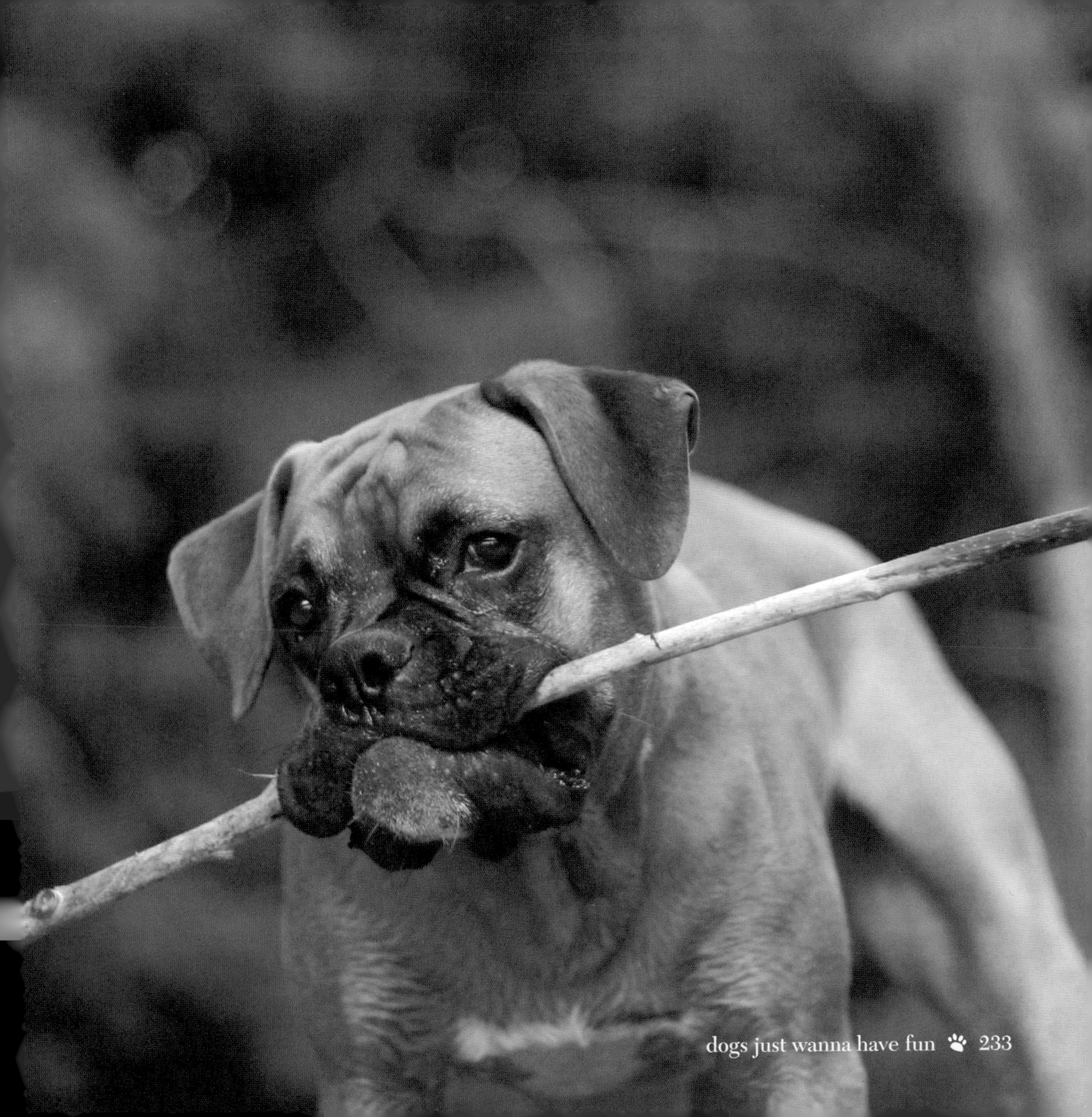

Who can resist such a happy dog?

This hound dances exuberantly, and there's no mistake when guessing her current mood. Everything a dog thinks and feels is translated through body language. When a dog is happy and enthusiastic, as this one obviously is, you'll know it. Conversely, if she's feeling blue, her sad expression and lethargic behavior will give her away.

"This must be the trick....

Where's the treat?"

Famous Movie Dogs

Rin Tin Tin
(German Shepherd Dog)

Lassie (Collie)

Benji (mix)

Toto (Cairn Terrier)

Petey (Pit Bull)

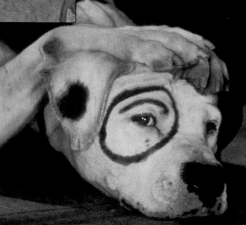

Old Yeller (mix)

Beethoven (St. Bernard)

Hooch (Dogue de Bordeaux)

Asta (Wirehaired Fox Terrier)

Bullet (German Shepherd Dog)

"It is fatal to let any dog know that he is funny, for he immediately loses his head and starts hamming it up."

—P. G. Wodehouse

"You first, Mikey! Test the water!"

Disc Dogs

Ashley Whippet, an appropriately named Whippet, kicked off a craze known as Disc Dogs by crashing a 1974 Major League Baseball pennant game between the Los Angeles Dodgers and the Cincinatti Reds. The dog's prowess was televised, and 50,000 fans cheered him on before he and his owner, Alex Stein, were run off the field. After that nonscheduled appearance (which landed Alex in jail with a fine), the two had several high-profile performances on *Monday Night Football, Wide World of Sports*, the Rose Bowl, and Super Bowl XII. They were invited to *The Tonight Show*—and even to the White House!

Ashley's talent and his high-profile debut rocketed the sport of Catch and Fetch to new heights of public awareness and popularity.

The canine flying disk world championship competition is called the Ashley Whippet Invitational. Owners play in their yards, in parks, and in competition. You can even get training videos. As with any other sport, dogs should be healthy and eager to participate.

This early film still of **Rin Tin Tin,** or "Rinty" as he was often called, shows the canine star with William Collier, Jr., in *The Lighthouse by the Sea.* The handsome German Shepherd Dog starred in silent and sound movies in the 1920s and 1930s—he even had his own radio show and captured the hearts of children and adults alike. His descendents kept the Rin Tin Tin name alive in movies and TV shows for many years.

Hairiest Dogs
(longest hair)

Skye Terrier

Komondor

Puli

Bearded Collie

Lhasa Apso

Tibetan Terrier

Maltese

Pekingese

Yorkshire Terrier

Shih Tzu

Ta da! Not only are dogs great swimmers, but they're great divers, too. It doesn't take much to motivate a dog to dive in. Toss a ball or a favorite toy and—splash! Dogs will leap off a pier or even a cliff. This dog seems to have nothing in mind beyond retrieving whatever object was thrown.

For some dogs, *there's nothing like getting wet.* And if the body of water is a river, that's even better. With miles of shore to explore, a dog can spend hours splashing, running, sniffing, and swimming. It may be best not to take a water-loving dog fishing, though. He simply won't be able to sit quietly on shore waiting for a bite!

Swimming Dos and Don'ts

-Most dogs love to swim. They just jump in and start paddling—hence the phrase "dog paddle." Others are a bit more leery about diving in head first. People who want to encourage their dogs to join the watery fun can do so by splashing and making inviting noises or by throwing a toy into the water—just be sure it floats.

Some dogs can develop ear infections if they spend too much time in the water. Be sure to wipe their ears out thoroughly when the fun is done. Keep your dog out of streams and creeks, and especially do not allow him to drink from them, due to the danger of parasites.

Every year, dogs drown in swimming pools. Although most dogs happily paddle about, they usually can't find a way to exit the pool when they tire. If you plan to allow your dog around the pool—or in case the gates are accidentally left open—show him how to climb the ladder or place a ramp in the pool, so the dog can climb out safely. Also, pets sometimes drown in the off-season if they decide to take a walk on the pool cover. It can sink and drag the dog down, making it impossible for him to escape.

Swimming in a warm pool is good therapy for dogs who have aching joints or are recovering from injuries. And it's as beneficial for dogs who need to lose weight or get into better shape as it is for people!

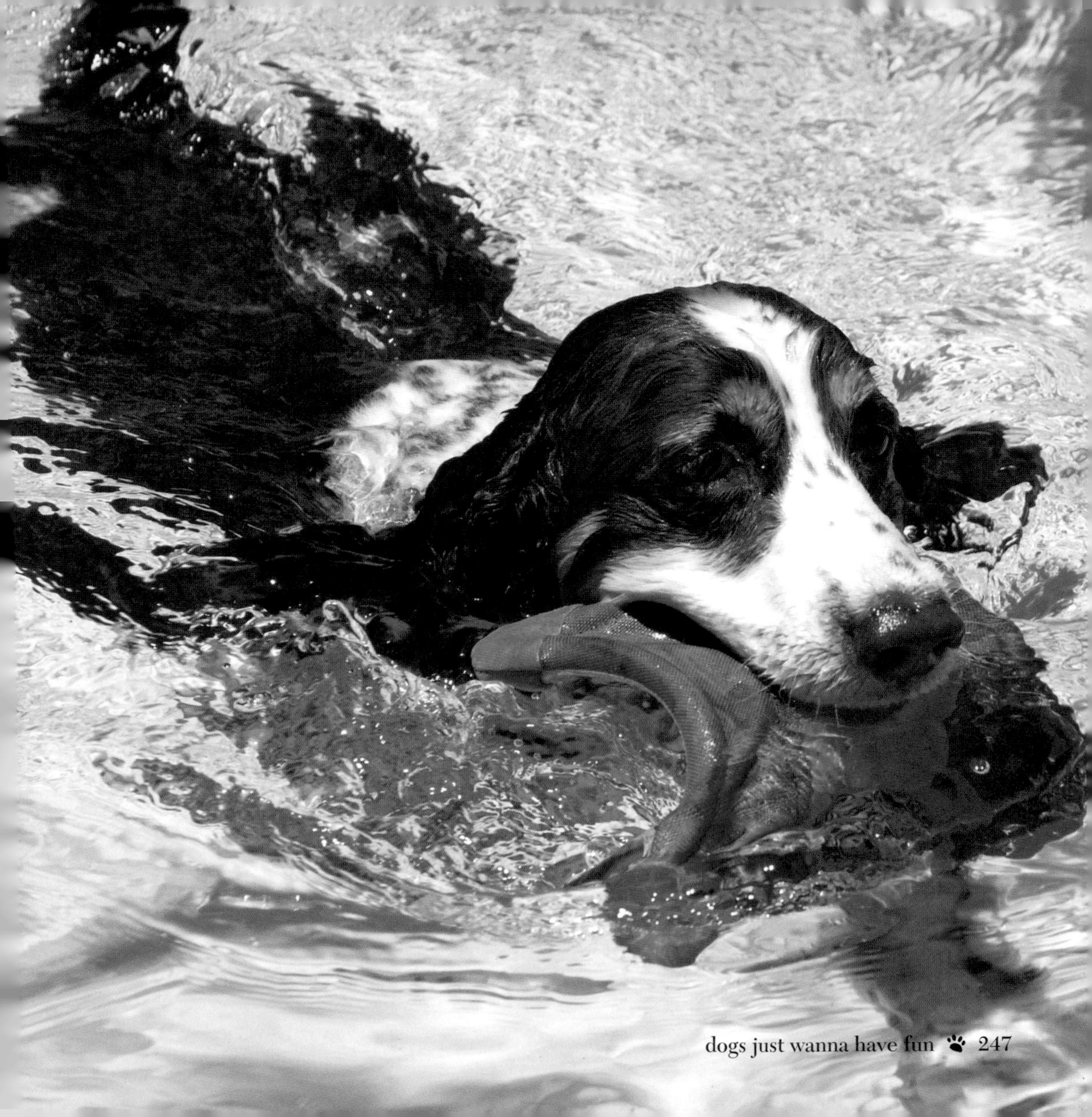

A Woofin' Good Time!

Fun at Home

Swimming

Running

Digging

Hide-and-Seek

Treasure hunts

Fetching------------

Hiking

Tug------------

Keep away------------

Trail rides

GAMES AT HOME

Great for teaching your dog to use her nose for tracking or just for fun, hide-and-seek

is one of the simplest games people and dogs can enjoy. The dog should have a solid stay, or her collar should be held by another person. Start by having the dog find something over a short distance—around a corner or in the next room. Eventually, you can build up to searching over longer distances or in a wooded area. The greatest successes come when the dog learns to use her nose instead of by following a voice.

"We call him George Maestro Handel. He thinks he's a conductor, wags his tail constantly as if every direction he turns he's got an orchestra back there."

—D. C. Berry

Cartoon Dogs

Deputy Dawg

Snoopy

Astro

Underdog

Huckleberry Hound

Lady & Tramp- - - - - - - - - - - - - - - -┐

Goofy- - - - - - - - - - - - - - - - ┐   │

Ren   │

Augie Doggie & Doggy Daddy   │

Scooby Doo   │

Pluto- - - - - - - - ┐   │

Arliss Coates (played by Kevin Corcoran) lies in bed with **Old Yeller,** the stray dog who came to live with his Texas family in 1869. *Old Yeller* was released Christmas Day, 1957, and was extremely successful. This three-hankie tearjerker received glowing reviews from critics and continues to be cherished by generations of dog lovers.

"I didn't do it! He did it!"

Lure Coursing

Sighthounds love to run, and they were born to chase rabbits and other small animals. Lure coursing events are held in open fields. They usually involve three dogs running a lap, chasing the "bunny," which nowadays is a plastic bag or mechanical lure. The dogs are scored on agility, following, enthusiasm, speed, and endurance.

Most competitions use a motorized lure machine with a long line (up to 1,200 yards). Courses are laid out in various patterns, with the dogs zigging and zagging to catch that "bunny."

"Splish, splash, I was taking a bath." And from the looks of this dog's enthusiastic shaking, whoever is standing nearby is just as wet as she is! Some dogs accept bathtime quite gracefully, but others are eager to share the wet, soapy festivities with their best two-legged friend. Owners should keep in mind that this good, clean fun is meant in the spirit of play.

Whether alone or with friends, this dog knows *there's nothing like playing in the surf.* The constant ebbs and flows are a mystery to the canine mind, which makes it all the more fun. When the water goes out, there are all kinds of creatures to chase and all sorts of scents to smell. And when the water comes in, it's delightful to run and splash in the waves.

GAMES AT HOME

Dogs enjoy playing

tug-of-war

with people and with

other dogs. Care should be taken that the dog doesn't become

aggressive about the tug, however. If that happens, the tug should be

put away. Dogs should be taught to "give" when commanded to do

so. This simple training can be accomplished by giving a treat at the

release word.

"No, because if I 'drop it,' you're just going to throw it again."

Hairiest Dogs
(poufiest hair)

Old English Sheepdog

Chow Chow

Pomeranian

Keeshond

Samoyed

Poodle

Collie

Komondor

Puli

Pekingese

"I know you're in here somewhere!"

Big Air Dogs

These dogs make spectacular jumps by running off docks and leaping into the water. The dogs with the longest jumps are the winners. Begun as friendly competition between owners and their dogs, it became an actual performance event in 2000. The governing body, with rules based on track and long jump field events, is called DockDogs. Although any breed can participate, retrievers excel. Little Morgan, a black Labrador, was the record holder in 2005 with a jump of 26'6"!

In the competition, the handler throws a floating object (maybe a dummy, a ball, or a disk) into the water, and the dog, with a 40-foot running start, leaps off the dock to retrieve it. Top contenders usually jump more than 20 feet. Measurements are made with laser sighting and digital video equipment.

It's a fun event for spectators and competitors. And the dogs—well, they're flying high with excitement!

This dog flies through the air in the qualifying rounds of a dog dive competition.

EAST COAST WAREHOUSE II

14 13 12 11 10 9 8 7 6

Most people have a favorite character from *The Wizard of Oz*, but Dorothy (Judy Garland) and Toto are probably the two best loved by audiences. Toto, a cute, scrappy Cairn Terrier, was perfect for his part in the movie. It's difficult to imagine another breed sharp enough to outsmart a wizard and a wicked witch.

GAMES AT HOME

Hide a treat or favorite toy under a cup or other container, and spread other empty containers around. Encourage your dog to use her nose to find the reward in a kind of **treasure hunt.** It's fun to see just how quickly your dog can hone in on the correct container. Some dogs will be better at this than others, but every dog can improve with practice.

Comic-al Dogs

Marmaduke

Daisy (*Blondie*)

Snoopy (*Peanuts*)

Odie (*Garfield*)

Sandy (*Little Orphan Annie*)

Electra and Vivian (*Cathy*)

Krypto (*Superman*)

Otto (*Beetle Bailey*)

Dogbert (*Dilbert*)

Doggie (*Zippy*)

Grimmy (*Mother Goose and Grimm*)

Dogzilla (*The Buckets*)

Fred Basset

Dollar the Dog (*Richie Rich*)

Farley and Edgar (*For Better or for Worse*)

Puddles (*Luann*)

Satchell (*Get Fuzzy*)

Snert (*Hagar the Horrible*)

Buckles

Ruff (*Dennis the Menace*)

Bullet (*Snuffy Smith*)

Dawg (*Hi and Lois*)

Rex, the Wonder Dog

Homer (*Crankshaft*)

Earl (*Mutts*)

Fifi (*Bringing Up Father*)

Though Greyhound racing is a controversial sport, there's no doubt the breed is fast and well suited for the activity. Once retired from the track, Greyhounds make excellent pets and devoted companions. They are playful, intelligent friends who are especially fun to take for a walk. Because people associate Greyhounds with racing, seeing one walking in the neighborhood can be an unexpected treat.

"You don't know what you can get away with *until you try.*"
—Colin Powell

Flyball

Flyball is a relay race between two or more teams, with four dogs on each team. In the competition, the dogs must jump over four hurdles (the height of which is determined by the smallest dog on the team) to reach a spring-loaded box. At the box, the dog must step on a release and then catch a tennis ball that has been launched into the air. When the dog has raced back over the hurdles with the ball in its mouth, the next dog on the team is released to run the same course. Throughout the race, dogs must stay on course, they must not drop the ball, and they cannot cross over to the other team. This last rule can be a tall order, because seeing other running dogs with balls in their mouths is sometimes too tempting for a canine competitor! If a dog gets distracted from the course, he must run it again.

As you can probably guess, this sport is fast, noisy, and highly energetic! Dogs waiting thier turn bark their enthusiasm and must be restrained by a handler until time for their release. The handlers and spectators also encourage the dogs by cheering them on. The winning team is the one in which all four dogs run the fastest time without errors. The record score is 15.43 seconds!

As if catching a flying disc wasn't difficult enough with two hands—

how about catching one with your mouth? To dogs, it's

all in a day's work—or more accurately, a day's fun. Tossing a disc for

Fido has progressed from a simple owner-and-dog activity to a

highly competitive sport. Canine disc competitions, which take place

all over the United States, are awesome to watch.

Lassie's fame began with the book by Eric Knight. A film version, Lassie Come Home, *kicked off decades of screen popularity for the beloved Collie. The first television series had one of the longest runs ever—17 years.*

Famous Dog Quiz

1. What TV show had a ghostly canine?

2. Name the dog on *Frasier.*

3. Who belonged to Constable Benton Fraser on *Due South*?

4. Who was the canine member of *The Partridge Family*?

5. Who was "The Dog Who Saved Hollywood"?

Enzo the dog went by another name on Frasier.

6. What is Nipper's claim to fame?

7. What was the name of the Old English Sheepdog on *Please Don't Eat the Daisies*?

8. What dog ran with *The Bionic Woman*?

9. What animal, part dog and part wolf, starred in a novel by Jack London?

10. What was the name of *My Three Sons'* canine cast member?

Answers: 1. *Topper,* 2. Eddie, 3. Diefenbaker, 4. Simone, 5. Won Ton, 6. He's listening to his master's voice on the RCA logo, 7. Ladadog, 8. Max, 9. White Fang, 10. Tramp

GAMES AT HOME

Certainly the most common game to play with dogs is **fetch,** which consists of simply throwing a ball, a stick, or another retrievable item

and encouraging the dog to chase after it and bring it back (most dogs don't need very much encouragement). This is a favorite of almost every dog. In fact, the person will usually tire long before the dog will! Fetch also serves to bring about a kind of bonding between dogs and their humans.

"I ran. I got the ball. I brought it back. Now what?"

"Dogs feel very strongly that they should always go with you in the car, in case the need should arise for them to bark violently at nothing right in your ear."

—Dave Barry

"These aren't wrinkles—they're laugh lines!"

dog tails & talents

"*My little dog*—a heartbeat at my feet."

—Edith Wharton

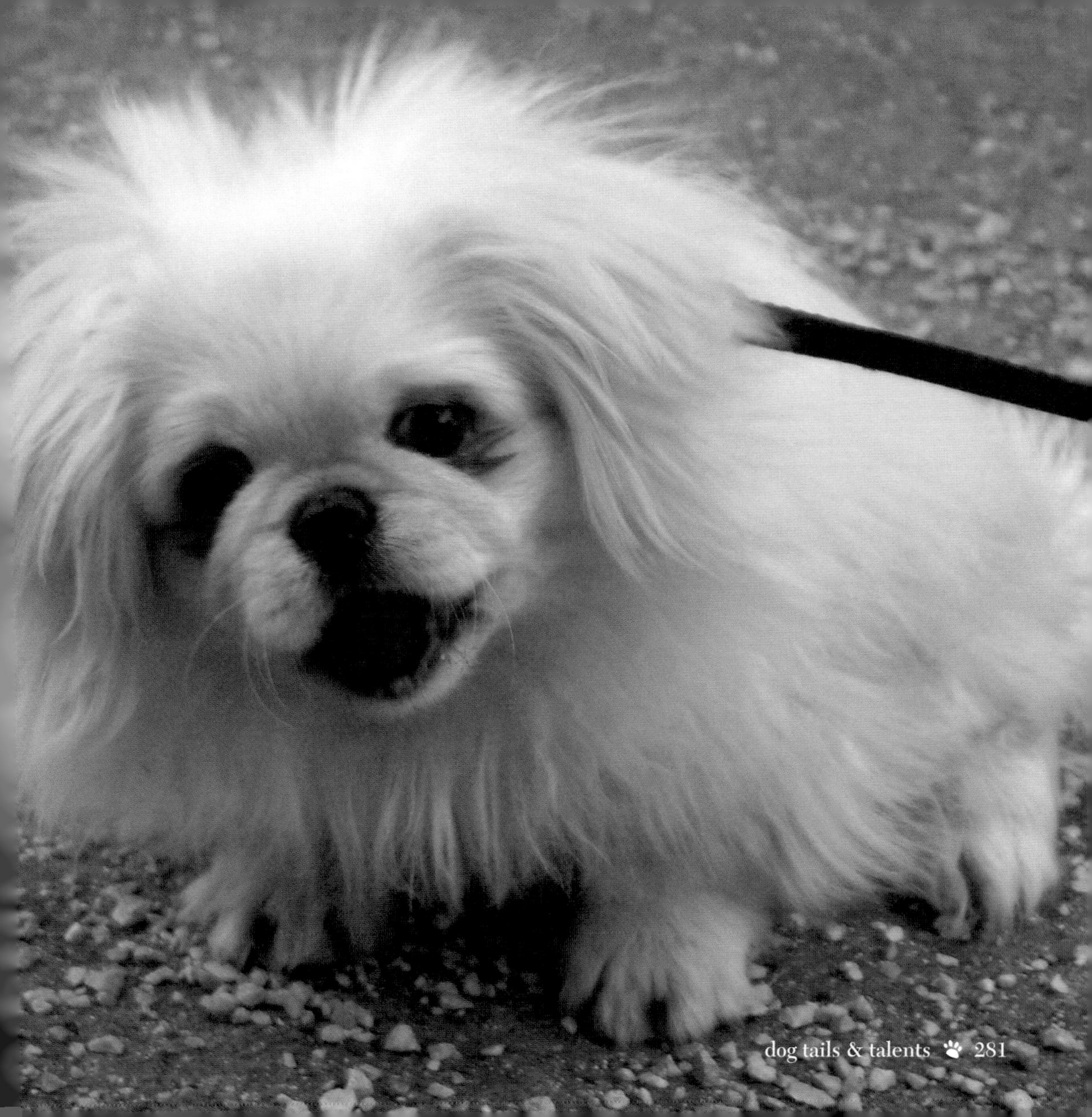

True Love

If ever

I find a man

Who follows me
   willingly,

Looks at me daily
   with devotion,

Kisses my hand and
   my tears,

And wags his tail with
   joy at my approach,

I won't need a dog.

1 **Whippets** were bred to be racers. Known for their swiftness, they have a top speed of 37 miles per hour.

2 **Greyhounds** can hit the speed limit of 45 miles per hour for short spurts!

3 **Dalmatian puppies and Australian Cattledogs** are pure white at birth. Freckles and spots appear later.

Whippet

4 **Dogs age more quickly** than people, but it's not at the rate of seven dog years for one human year. The first year is actually equivalent to about 16 years—yes, they go from babies to teenagers that quickly! At two years old, they're about the same as a person at 24—through school, settling down, and thinking about getting married. At three years old, they're equivalent to about 30 in human years. After that, they age at about the equivalent of five years to every one they live.

Amazing Archie

Archie, a black Labrador, became separated from his master at the train station near Aberdeen, Scotland. Closed-circuit television showed the dog waiting patiently for quite some time for his owner, Mike Taitt, to return. When the owner didn't show up, the dog went for the next best thing—taking the train home by himself. Not only did he get on the correct train, but he got off at the correct stop. That's something a lot of *people* have trouble doing!

The greatest nurse

is the one with the most patience.

"Heaven goes by favor. If it went by merit, you would stay out and your dog would go in."

—Mark Twain

Eternal Wait

Hachiko, an Akita, walked to the train every day with Dr. Eisaburo Ueno, a professor at Tokyo University. Every night, loyal Hachiko greeted the professor when he arrived home. Unfortunately, the man died at work one day. Hachiko, always faithful and always waiting, was at the train station every day for

the next nine years until his own death. Dog lovers around the world so admired his faithfulness that they made donations to erect a statue to the loyal dog at the Shibuya railroad station in Tokyo.

Rarest Dogs

Lundehund

Canadian Eskimo Dog

Patterdale Terrier

Telomian Dog

Cesky Terrier

New Guinea Singing Dog

Chinook

Xoloitzcuintli

Thai Ridgeback

Tahltan Bear Dog

Dancing with Dogs

Canine Freestyle is choreographed movement with your dog. No, the dancing isn't like holding a human partner in your arms, but it's fun to watch or to dance. A routine is designed with the human and canine partners performing to music. Subtle vocal or hand commands signal the dog to spin, weave, back up, or rise on his hind legs. When performed in competition, scoring is done on grace, precision, and artistic talent. This activity was originally based on a combination of dressage and obedience. The teamwork is amazing and demonstrates the bond between handler and dog.

Old Bob, Ghost Dog

Irene suffered a stroke, and her 14-year-old daughter helped care for her at their home in Liverpool, England. The following year, Irene was better, and she convinced her daughter to go on a school trip to France.

While Irene was alone, two burglars broke into the house. In hiding from the intruders, Irene heard growls and a cry. A neighbor also heard the commotion and alerted the police, who arrived and arrested the burglars. The police told Irene that her dog had frightened the intruders and had even bitten one. Irene replied that she once had an Alsatian (German Shepherd Dog) named Bob, but he had died 14 years earlier. Later that night Irene heard nails on the floor and felt a cold, wet nose poke her as she lay in bed. She opened her eyes to see Bob, her old dog, protecting her once more. Bob vanished when Irene reached out to pet his snout.

When Irene's daughter returned home, she took a picture of her mother in the garden. When they picked up the developed photos, an out-of-focus dog could be seen sitting with Irene. It was Bob, her faithful friend.

"We thought these costumes would help clarify who's in charge around here."

Dogs Dig Digging!

Although many dogs want to visit China the hard way, certain breeds just get a thrill out of digging! If you're a persnickety gardener or lawn proud, it might be best to steer your terriers and other wannabe gardeners to a particular area they can call their own. Fence in your dog, or fence in your garden—either way, find a place where your dog can simply be a dog. If you have a determined digger trying to escape your yard, sink mesh below your fence—the more doggedly they dig, the deeper the mesh should be.

Digging is a favorite canine activity. The flying dirt provides entertainment, and the resulting hole can be a good hiding place for a bone or a cool bed in which to escape summer's heat. Nordic breeds such as the Samoyed enjoy digging, even though it is unlikely that today's dog would need to scrape out a cozy nest in the snow the way their ancestors once did.

Service Dogs

- Under the Americans with Disabilities Act, assistance, hearing, guide, and psychiatric service dogs all qualify to accompany their people everywhere, including at businesses, in restaurants, and on public transportation. They also may live in buildings that have "no pet" clauses, as they are not considered pets but therapeutic service animals. Therapy dogs, however, are not included in the act because they visit challenged persons rather than live with them.

- Dogs can also be very useful in helping sick people heal. Therapy dogs can make people feel better by doing what they do best: using their silly grins, wagging tails, and licking tongues to raise the spirits of ill patients. Therapy Dogs International, Inc., is probably the best-known organization offering certification for animals to be used in therapy.

- Therapy dogs also serve at disaster sites. They comfort victims and their families during what can be a long wait for aid. Many service dogs have been inducted into various halls of fame for their heroism and dedication.

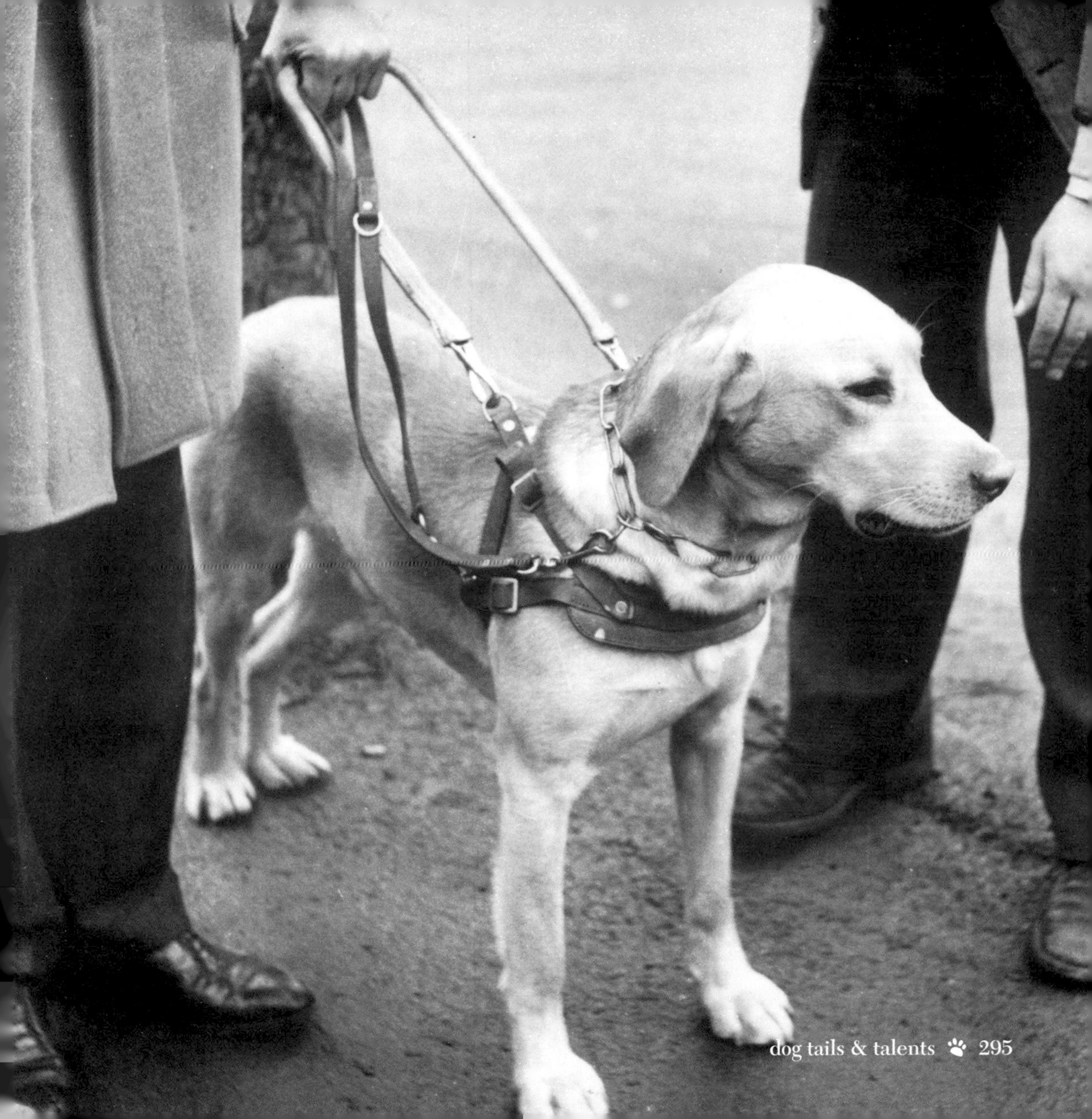

Morris and Essex

This show is as prestigious and proper as a lady's hat and gloves. In fact, many of the women wore this combination when attending early Morris and Essex dog shows. Conceived by Geraldine Rockefeller Dodge, who was a dog fancier and judge, the show was begun in 1927 at her Giralda Farms. It was held outdoors on the polo field until 1957. It truly was a world-class show, with gourmet luncheons, shining sterling silver trophies, and cash prizes.

Mrs. Dodge spared no expense in hosting the best judges in the world. In 1930, she brought the "father" of the German Shepherd Dog, Captain Max von Stephanitz, over from Germany to judge an entry of 275 Shepherds. Herr Gustav Alisch, known as "Mr. Dachshund," came from Germany in 1936 to judge the Dachshund Club of American specialty held at M & E. He drew a record entry of 311 Dachshunds.

The show had a rebirth in 2000 with an outstanding entry of 3,000 dogs. Plans are to hold it every five years on the beautiful grounds of Colonial Park in Somerset, New Jersey. Several of the current judges harken to the styles of yesteryear by wearing their fanciest chapeaus. They are served an elegant lunch on linen and fine china.

Rico, the Canine Dictionary

Rico, a Border Collie from Germany, understands 200 words. He was tested by a psychologist, Dr. Juliane Kaminski of the Max Planck Institute for Evolutionary Anthropology. Rico is thought to have the same language skills as trained apes, dolphins, parrots, and sea lions. The dog can also apply simple logic by picking out the right object when told to do so. When a new object with a strange word is added, he can even figure out which one that is!

His owners began teaching him the names of his toys when he was a puppy to keep him from being bored. He did his homework awfully well!

Dogs That Wag Their Behinds

Polish Lowland Sheepdog

Boxer

Australian Shepherd

Pembroke Welsh Corgi

Old English Sheepdog

Schnauzer (Giant, Standard, and Mini)

Rottweiler

Doberman Pinscher

Miniature Pinscher

German Pinscher

Legendary Dogs and Pseudo Dogs

- St. Guinefort was actually a Greyhound in Lyons, France. He was sainted because of his heroic rescue of a child from a rattlesnake in its cradle.

- According to legend, Asclepius, the Greek god of medicine, was saved from starvation by nursing on a bitch.

- Irish legend says that Setanta, the nephew and foster son of the king, killed a dog that belonged to a man named Cullan. The master was so grieved by the loss of his dog that the youth offered to serve as Cullan's hound until a replacement could be readied. He changed his name to Cuchullain, which means "the hound of Cullan."

This statue of Asclepius is a Roman copy of a Greek original.

"If I have any
beliefs about
immortality, it is
that certain dogs I
have known will
go to heaven, and
very, very few
persons."

—James Thurber

Bully for Patsy Ann!

Patsy Ann was popular in Juneau, Alaska, during the 1930s. The Bull Terrier greeted every ship that docked at the port and so was named the Official Greeter of Juneau. In those days, dogs often wandered about towns, and Patsy Ann spent her spare time going from business to business.

She became a bit chubby due to all the treats from the locals and the ships' cooks. She spent her nights in the Longshoreman's Hall, surrounded by her friends. When she died, a statue of her was erected to watch over the Gastineau Channel.

Listening as Well as Talking

Dax, an eleven-year-old Australian Shepherd, and his owner, Elizabeth, have been visiting an assisted living facility for several years. One of their favorite gentlemen is John, a retired engineer. He always has stories of his younger years, projects he's worked on, his kids and their families, and of course, his favorite subject: dogs. One day when Dax and his owner arrived, John's family was there visiting with him, so Elizabeth said, "I don't want to intrude; we'll come back later." But one of John's relatives quickly responded, "No, no, come on in!"

As Elizabeth and Dax stepped in, John began introducing them to his family, who had surprised looks on their faces. Someone said, "Grandpa! You're talking!" Everyone began crowding around John. Elizabeth found out that John hadn't spoken to anyone in the family in several years.

She said, "But you've talked to Dax and me on every visit. What's up?"

He replied, "I love to talk about dogs, so I enjoy talking to you and Dax. And you're good listeners! But in this family, everyone likes to talk, and no one likes to listen!"

"*They never talk about themselves*

but listen to you while you talk about yourself, and keep up an

appearance of being interested in the conversation."

—Jerome K. Jerome

The close *relationship between this man and his canine guide is* based on *trust.* Traveling through a city, for example, requires an individual to rely on the dog's judgment of safe and unsafe conditions.

Because of this, great care is taken by trainers to match the right dog with the right person. The pair must "click"—the individual must feel comfortable with the dog and vice versa. Picking the right partner means the difference between success and failure.

Service dogs that aid the blind are probably the most widely recognized assistance dogs. Certified assistance dogs are allowed into all establishments and onto public transportation. Owners carry licenses to show that the dog is a necessary companion.

"**Dogs** are the *only creatures gifted to serve us* beyond the call of duty."

—C. W. Meisterfeld

Morris and Essex

- Geraldine Rockefeller Dodge owned as many as 80 different breeds of dogs in her lifetime.

- Mrs. Dodge was the principal person responsible for dividing American and English Cockers. A few other Cocker fanciers joined her in the quest to have English Cockers recognized as a separate breed, which finally came to pass in 1946.

- Morris and Essex was not truly an all-breed show. Each year Mrs. Dodge would select various breeds in each group to have classes at the show.

- Mrs. Dodge personally offered trophies for each breed in honor of each judge.

- Guests were served boxed lunches by uniformed waiters.

- Today, classic cars of the bygone era add to the glamour of yesteryear.

- Mrs. Dodge used her considerable wealth to benefit others. In keeping with this tradition, M & E donates proceeds of the show to the University of Pennsylvania School of Veterinary Medicine, Cornell College of Veterinary Medicine, the American Kennel Club Canine Health Foundation, and St. Hubert's Giralda, an animal shelter founded by Mrs. Dodge.

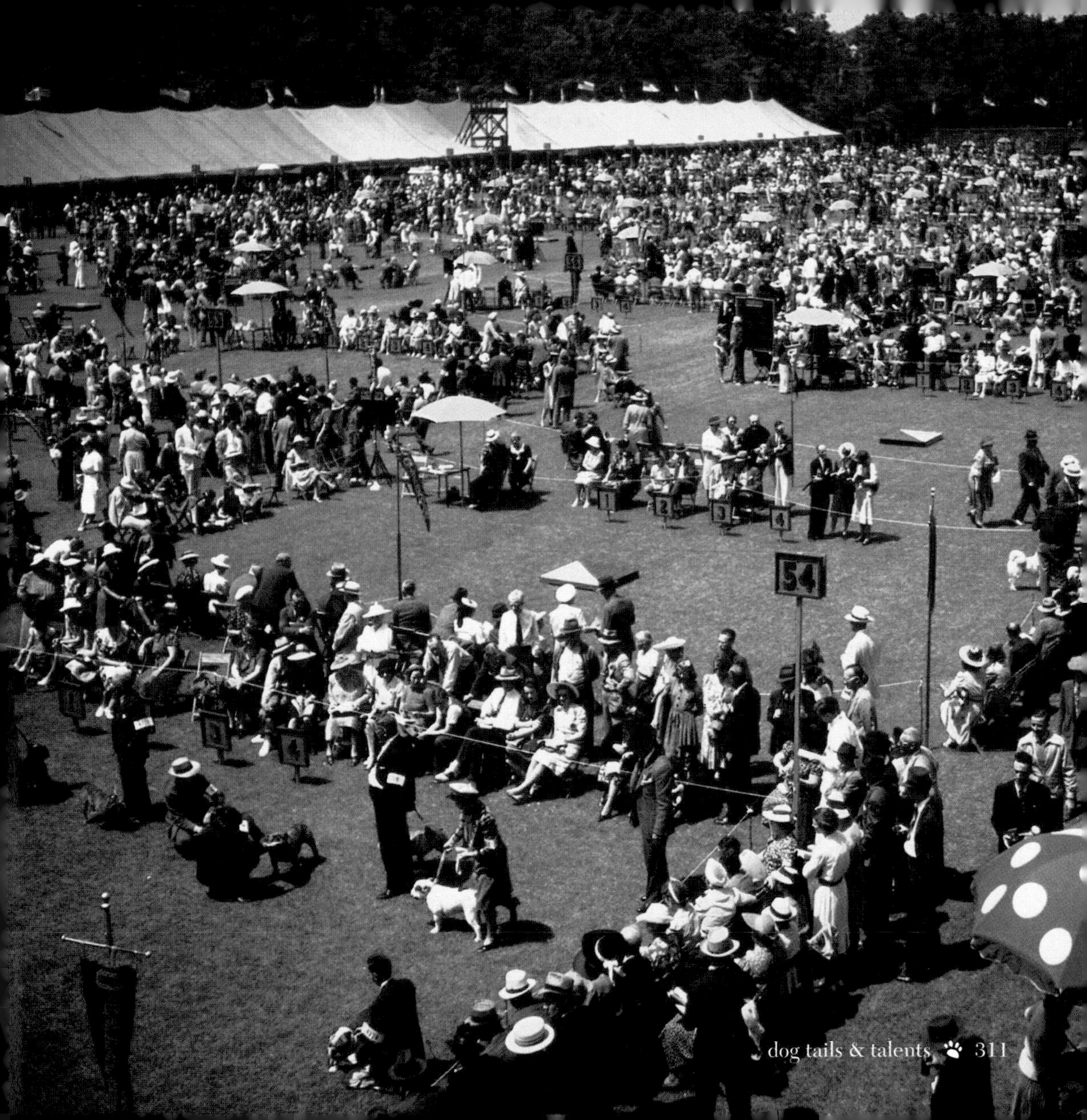
54

Marine Corps Mascot

For many years, the U.S. Marine Corps has had an unofficial mascot, a Bulldog named Private Jiggs. He was quickly promoted to corporal, then sergeant, and then sergeant major, due to his dogged attentiveness to duty. After his passing, other Bulldogs have always held a place of honor in the Marines, some named Jiggs, others named Smedly after a general. Since the 1950s, all Marine Corps Bulldogs have been named Chesty, honoring Lieutenant General Lew B. "Chesty" Puller, Jr. The dogs, in full uniform, often accompany the Marines in parades. They are a symbol of the determination and courage of the Marines.

We are their gods—so can we be any less?

The wind in your hair. A dog in your backpack. *Life just doesn't get much better than this.*

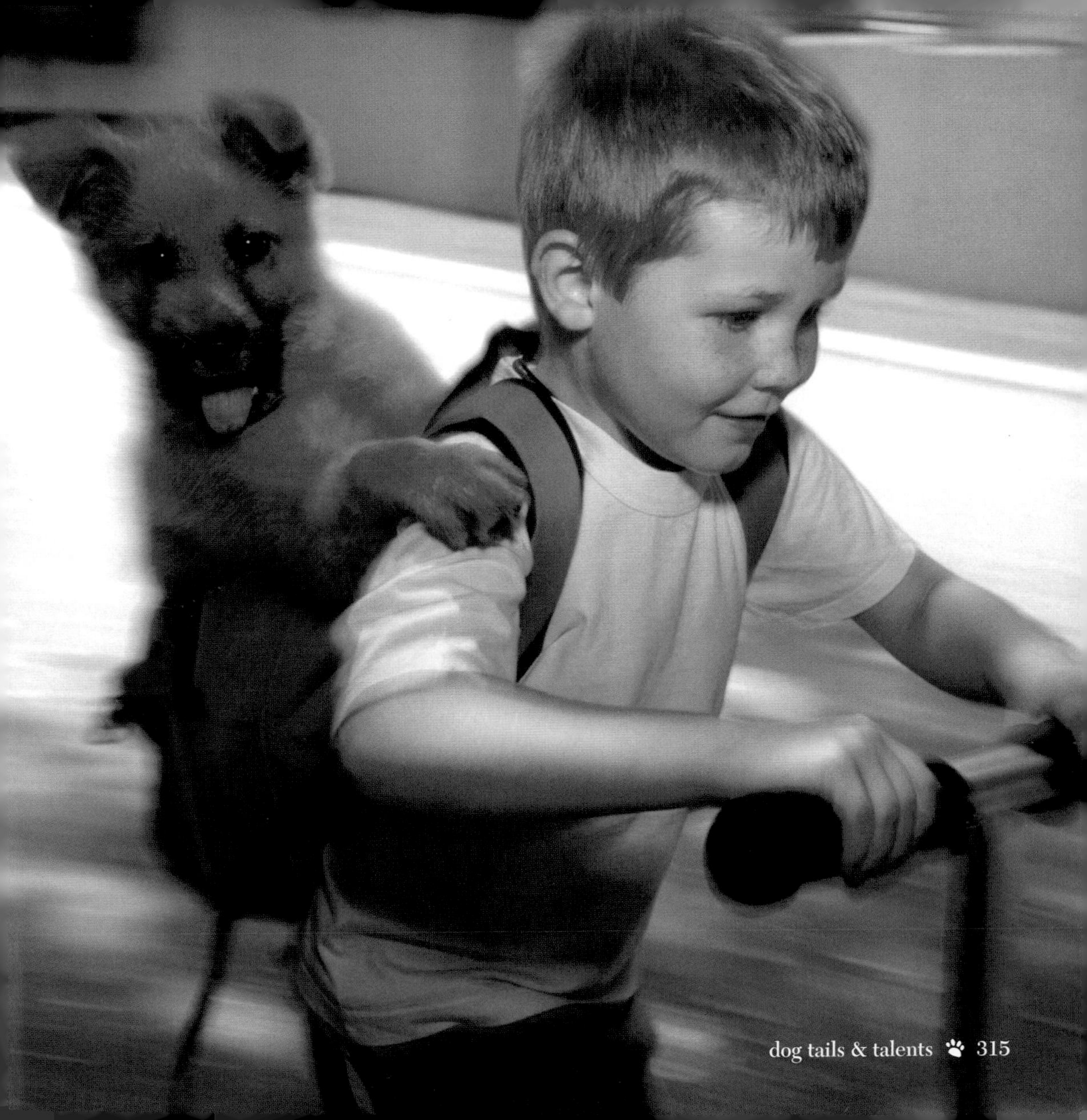

index